Tony's Guide

to the courier industry

by Tim Gilbert

Note for Librarians: a cataloguing record for this book that includes Dewey Decimal Classification and US Library of Congress numbers is available from the Library and Archives of Canada. The complete cataloguing record can be obtained from their online database at:
www.collectionscanada.ca/amicus/index-e.html
ISBN 1-4120-2400-5

Printed in Victoria, BC, Canada

 Printed on paper with minimum 30% recycled fibre. Trafford's print shop runs on "green energy" from solar, wind and other environmentally-friendly power sources.

Offices in Canada, USA, Ireland and UK

This book was published *on-demand* in cooperation with Trafford Publishing. On-demand publishing is a unique process and service of making a book available for retail sale to the public taking advantage of on-demand manufacturing and Internet marketing. On-demand publishing includes promotions, retail sales, manufacturing, order fulfilment, accounting and collecting royalties on behalf of the author.

Book sales for North America and international:
Trafford Publishing, 6E–2333 Government St.,
Victoria, BC v8t 4p4 CANADA
phone 250 383 6864 (toll-free 1 888 232 4444)
fax 250 383 6804; email to orders@trafford.com

Book sales in Europe:
Trafford Publishing (uk) Ltd., Enterprise House, Wistaston Road Business Centre,
Wistaston Road, Crewe, Cheshire cw2 7rp UNITED KINGDOM
phone 01270 251 396 (local rate 0845 230 9601)
facsimile 01270 254 983; orders.uk@trafford.com
Order online at:
trafford.com/04-0228

10 9 8 7 6 5 4

Tony's Guide

to the courier industry

This book is dedicated to all the brilliant courier people whose ideas have contributed to it over the years.

With thanks to Marjorie Gilbert.

Tony's Guide

to the courier industry

Tony's Guide
to the courier industry

This book will help you achieve your personal goals in the courier industry.

If you are aiming to start out as an owner driver (sometimes called a "freelance courier") in this industry, this book will help you get started along the right lines. The early sections are for you. Then when you want to move on up to getting your own customers, the rest of the book will help you develop your skills.

If you're an "old hand" at being a courier, this book will keep you abreast of the latest developments in the industry, to allow you to make the most of your valuable experience.

If you're aiming to grow your existing courier business, this whole book can be used as a kind of operating manual for your business, to guide you through the many pitfalls along the way.

Useful to just about everyone in the courier industry, this book will also help you to apply some or all of the features on MTvan.com to your business. Packed with a wealth of tried and trusted ideas and information, this book will help you to get the most out of your business.

Who is Tony? Tony has been one of the guiding lights behind MTvan.com. He moderates on the MTvan Forum.

And who is Tim Gilbert? Founder of MTvan.com and founder committee member of the Despatch Association, Tim has been at the forefront of new ideas in the courier industry for over 25 years.

© Tim Gilbert 2005

Tony's Guide

to the courier industry

Tony's Guide | to the courier industry

The Same-Day Express Courier Market

Let's first of all be quite clear what we mean by "courier" in this book. It's a "same day courier". It's the kind of courier who collects from a business customer immediately in a small van, and goes straight to the delivery point and gets a signature. Like a minicab for parcels. There are some variations on this theme, but this description makes it clear that we are not talking about couriers or carriers like Parcelforce, who generally collect towards the end of the day, to take parcels to the local depot for delivery overnight by means of a system of depots, vehicles, and even aeroplanes, operating through the night.

We firmly believe that this same day courier market will remain worthwhile for many years to come.

We think that the market will continue to grow, driven by the increase in pace of the economy generally. Everything happens and changes faster nowadays, so instant delivery is only going to become more essential.

Most of what is being carried now and in the future will be "product" ie stuff which you can't send via email.

This growth is attracting big names into the market. Big brands such as DHL Express and Business Post are now getting a real foothold in this market, which a few years ago they almost completely ignored.

All this means that there's a bright future, especially for really reliable and approved owner-drivers. Smaller courier company players, to compete, will need to offer something even more special to their

© Tim Gilbert 2005

Tony's Guide
to the courier industry

customers such as really meticulous customer care, which larger
companies often find difficult to deliver locally.

That's as well as everyone having to offer an increasingly high level of
"the basics", such as accurate delivery, smart vans with professionally
turned-out drivers, instant Proof of Delivery information on the web,
on-line bookings and enquiries, instant national coverage, 24/7
availability, consistent pricing, electronic invoicing, and performance
reporting.

This guide can help you to get the most out of this market, even as
these exciting changes are taking place.

What's involved in becoming a courier? 3

This section describes the minimum standards expected by same-day courier companies offering an express delivery service throughout the UK.

If you're planning to make a living as an owner-driver courier, the best way to start is to find work with courier companies in your area. The following sections will help you know what they expect.

The range of customers using these courier companies is very broad but typically customers are solicitors, accountants, advertising and PR companies, printers, building contractors, engineering companies, and so on. In fact anyone who needs something collecting and delivering immediately.

Courier companies need couriers like you to carry out the work, so it's the obvious place to start.

You can contact courier companies throughout the UK, and especially your local ones, through MTvan.com. Just type into the search box the town names of places within easy reach of where you live, and call them. Arrange to pop in, if you can, for a quick chat, and to show them your van and your documents, and above all, to let them get to know you.

We recommend getting yourself a full listing on the "Find a Courier" section, including a photograph and all the details of your Goods in Transit and Public Liability Insurance. Use "Update my details" to do this:

© Tim Gilbert 2005

```
Find a courier

Courier Name         [                ]
Town or City         [                ]

You can search using at least two letters in one or both boxes:

Update your own details:                    Search
                                            (Update)
```

This extra information makes it easier for other members to feel that they can trust you to carry out their work. In the FAQs section at the back of this Guide, there's an example of how it will look.

Similarly, register with the MTvan Forum, and introduce yourself. This will help people feel they "know you". People do business with people they like, so give as many people as possible the chance to know and like you. Don't emphasise the fact that you're "new", rather that you're "available":

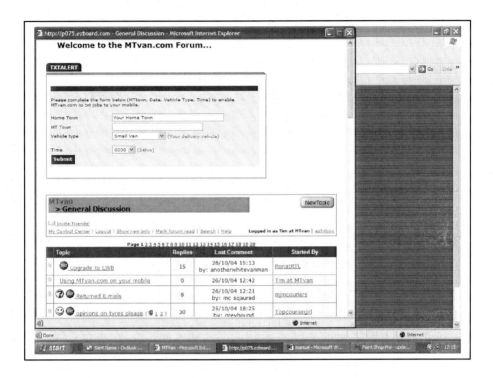

Then phone up all the courier companies in the Find a Courier within 50 miles of you, and introduce yourself, mentioning that you're a Member of MTvan.com so they can look you up.

Ask them to consider you for work, either overflow or regular. Some of them will ask you to turn up to see them, others will ask you to write in, others will say "I'll keep your number on file". They're the ones who may need several friendly phone calls to encourage them to remember you're there.

Get the fax number of those who sound interested, and fax them your Goods in Transit insurance certificate, and a covering letter including a photograph of you and your smart clean van. It's all a worthwhile investment. Contact especially any controller or Member who seems to be quite "high profile" on MTvan.com, and get to know them and what they need.

We strongly advise against sending letters out to all and sundry without phoning first. All you'll do is waste paper and postage, and worse still, you risk annoying people with your pointless junk mail.

To get yourself noticed, it's also worth bidding for any work you think you can reasonably do, from the Courier Work page. There are no rules on pricing. Just bid the lowest amount you are happy to do the job for. The more jobs you bid for, the more people will have your phone number to call on next time they're busy. And if your price is right, and they feel they can trust you, they might even give you the job.

Have a look at the "TxtMeMT" section of MTvan.com. Used regularly, this will get your name and phone number and location in front of controllers throughout the UK, for use when they're busy in your area.

TxtMeMT is very simple. It allows anyone with a mobile phone to text details of their location to be read by anyone looking at the

TxtMeMT screen. It's just 160 characters of free text, starting with MT, for others to read. Like this:

16/09/04 14:55:55 W352
COLIN HOLLINGSHEAD MT NEWBURY NOW

TxtMeJobs does more. Using your pc, you enter details of where you will be empty (your "MTtown") and when. This allows MTvan.com to text to your mobile details of any booking which arises near your Home Town and your MTtown.

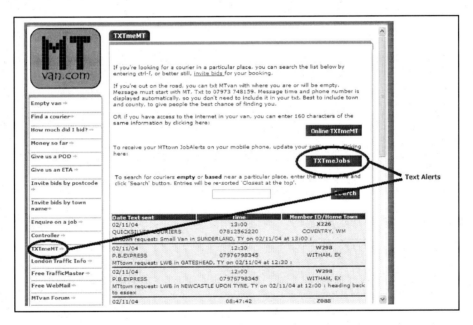

This gives you an opportunity to bid for work near your route. The details you enter will also appear on the TxtMeMT screen for others to see. Like this:

Tony's Guide
to the courier industry

16/09/04 20:00 X324 Greyhound Courier Service
MTtown request: LWB in BRISTOL, AV on 16/09/04 at 20:00

You will receive texts alerts of nearby courier work like this:

AI16729791 MTvan.com From SW19 on 16-09-04 Ready Now to
SUTTON, GL on 16-09-04 ASAP By TRANSIT- 01480 123456 2
pallets 50kg

You can reply to the phone number if there is one.

You cannot activate TxtMeJobs via your mobile, but we suggest you
enter details of where you are heading on TxtMeJobs using your PC
before you leave home, then txt your progress to TxtMeMT as you go
along:

Tony's Guide

to the courier industry

Tony's Guide

Look upon MTvan.com as a huge club of couriers and courier companies; people just like you who are building their own relationships in the same day courier business.

If you do all this, and especially if you "network" through MTvan.com as much as possible, you will soon have some work as an owner-driver courier. Once you've got a little, more will follow. It's all about how much you network with other members.

As soon as you have some work, ask the courier company to add you to their Trusted Members on Mtvan.com. This will help you, as it shows on your entry on Mtvan.com that you are a trusted member.

This helps others looking for a courier in your area, or checking you out before replying to your bid, to feel that they can trust you.

Tony's Guide

to the courier industry

The more trusted status you have, the higher up the list your entry shows to others, so you stand to get more business:

Find a courier

Click on 'more info' to see details of a courier's quality accreditations etc

Courier Co Name	Town Name	Tel Number
Courier's Name Member ID : W023 more info Track this member	BIRMINGHAM, WM Postcode: B23 Trusted by 8 Member(s)	Courier's Landline Courier's Mobile TM
Courier's Name Member ID : W397 more info Track this member	BIRMINGHAM, WM Postcode: B13 Trusted by 2 Member(s)	Courier's Landline Courier's Mobile TM
Courier's Name Member ID : W574 more info Track this member	BIRMINGHAM, WM Postcode: B27 Trusted by 1 Member(s)	Courier's Landline Courier's Mobile TM
Courier's Name Member ID : W536 more info Track this member	BIRMINGHAM, WM Postcode: B32 Trusted by 1 Member(s)	Courier's Landline Courier's Mobile TM
Courier's Name Member ID : X665 more info Track this member	BIRMINGHAM, WM Postcode: B36 Trusted by 1 Member(s)	Courier's Landline Courier's Mobile TM
Courier's Name Member ID : X278 more info Track this member	BIRMINGHAM, WM Postcode: B338	Courier's Landline Courier's Mobile Add to My Trusted Members
Courier's Name Member ID : X293 more info Track this member	BIRMINGHAM, WM Postcode: B46	Courier's Landline Courier's Mobile Add to My Trusted Members
Courier's Name Member ID : Z195 more info Track this member	BIRMINGHAM, WM Postcode: B34	Courier's Landline Courier's Mobile Add to My Trusted Members
Courier's Name Member ID : X711 more info Track this member	BIRMINGHAM, WM Postcode: B31A	Courier's Landline Courier's Mobile Add to My Trusted Members

Tony's Guide

As an owner-driver courier, you will be a self-employed subcontractor when working for the courier company. The relationship is similar to that between a householder and a plumber. The courier company (your customer) makes no deductions from your fee; you are paid a fee to get the job done, using your equipment, by any reasonable means at your disposal, and at your risk. Given the nature of this relationship with the courier company, you are responsible for your own income tax and national insurance contributions, as this is not a contract of employment.

As an owner-driver courier you are at liberty to work for more than one courier company. In fact, many courier companies positively encourage this, as if you only have one customer (the one courier company) it may be argued by the Inland Revenue that you are an employee. This would be bad for both you and especially for the courier company.

Working for several courier companies is easy if you make yourself available on MTvan.com, and bid for work from other courier members. Obviously, you have to avoid any risk of messing up work for one courier company because of work you're doing for another.

You need also to be very careful to look after the commercial secrets of all the courier companies you deliver for. You should take very seriously your own reputation for reliability, availability, discretion, and value. It'll take a long time to build it, and possibly seconds to destroy it.

Only ever promise what you can deliver, and once you've promised it, deliver it, and make sure the courier company knows you've delivered it.

As an owner-driver courier, you won't receive any payment to cover holidays or sickness. You are only paid for the delivery work you carry out, and you can choose your hours of availability yourself. Obviously, the more you're available, and the more helpful you are, the more work you'll be offered.

Tony's Guide
to the courier industry

Freelance couriers are typically paid an agreed percentage of whatever the courier company is charging the customer per job. Each company will advise you what the percentage is in your area and for your vehicle type. You should therefore enquire about their prices (to their customers), so you know what you're being paid a percentage of.

Rates to the customer vary by area and by van size, but generally a small van is charged out at between 75p and £1.10p per mile, and you'll be offered between 50% and 70% of that.

Of course, if you don't fancy the rate being offered, you're free to turn the work down or find work elsewhere. Generally, though, courier companies pay a reasonable rate (or they'd have no couriers) in return for reasonably quick payment (ideally 7 days, but sometimes up to a month).

To arrive at the price, mileage is calculated either from the collection point to the delivery point, or base to base. Each courier company will advise which is applicable in each case. Obviously the rate per mile will be lower if you are being paid base to base, than if you are being paid from collection to delivery.

You may well want to check the mileages being used.

You shouldn't become obsessed by them, as they can vary according to how you calculate them, but you should keep a check on them to ensure that any differences with your calculations are trivial, and that they're not always to your disadvantage.

If a job is a "wait and return", ie a two way trip collecting, delivering, waiting, collecting and returning to the original point, the return journey is usually charged and paid at a percentage of the one-way rate (which is typically 50% of the one-way rate). It's well worth asking about.

If you are kept waiting on a job, waiting time is paid. The rate usually varies depending on vehicle type. Each courier company will tell you the rates they charge and pay. Typically, for a wait of 15 minutes or less waiting time is usually not chargeable or payable, but if you wait for more than 15 minutes the wait is fully chargeable from when you started waiting.

Many courier companies pay weekly, a week in hand, by credit transfer, straight from their account to yours, or by cheque. You should of course receive a Customs & Excise approved self-billing invoice, which also acts as a pay advice detailing the work that you have done. Reputable companies will always give adequate documentation like this in support of payments made to you. If you're not getting some kind of list of what you're being paid for, and/or if you're not being asked to invoice the courier company, it's probably worth finding work elsewhere.

You may be expected to wear an ID Badge supplied by the courier company while on their business. We recommend that you also put together one of your own, with a photo, in the interests of professionalism. You could use a business card as an ID badge, with your photo on it, which can be obtained at modest cost from an online printer (see Deals and Discounts section of MTvan.com – there's even a template for you to use).

Dress code for a courier is typically smart black trousers (try to get the washable ones from places like Marks and Spencers that come out of the washing machine with the creases still smart and straight) and a white shirt or polo shirt. This allows you to really look the part while out delivering. Some courier companies may ask you to slip on an item of their clothing such as a sweatshirt or polo shirt while on their business.

This clothing bearing the courier company logo may even be sold to you. We recommend that you use your common sense here; if it seems like a sensible amount of money for the garment, and the company looks busy, it's probably worth it. If your instinct says it's an over priced rip-off, with no promise of work, you may want to go elsewhere.

Your van should typically be white in colour, and no more than 5 years old, and very clean inside and out. Many couriers find it actually pays them to rent (contract hire) a new van, rather than buy one outright and maintain it. Watch out for surcharges on excess mileages, though, as if you're successful, you'll be a high mileage user. (See Discounts and Deals section of MTvan.com for some ideas on Contract Hire).

Many courier companies offer their customers a 24-hour service, 365 days of the year, though most of the work comes in between 0800 and 2200 hrs Monday to Friday. This will vary depending on the courier company and on the nature of its contracts. Making yourself available out of office hours is often well worthwhile, as it makes you popular with the controllers (always a good thing, as they are the people who choose who gets which job) and the traffic is lighter (saves time and wear and tear) and the money is sometimes better per mile. Work booked outside office hours may be charged, and therefore paid, at higher rates. We suggest you ask about this.

How much money you will make subcontracting as an owner-driver courier to courier companies is impossible to predict, as there are so many factors involved. You can make anything from £250 in a week to £1500. The former figure is very low, probably less than 5 days' work, and the latter very high, almost certainly involving long hours and weekend work too. Since you get paid per job, the more you do, the more you get! If you do no work, you will get no money.

Just some of the issues which affect your income are shown below and most of them centre on your own efforts and abilities:

- ❏ Your aptitude for the work, how quickly and safely you can get from one place to another, how well you can navigate and read maps/GPS units etc.

- ❏ How many hours you are prepared to be available for work and how hard you are prepared to work during them. If you are unavailable to do early collections in the morning and want to finish on or before 1800 hours, you are obviously limiting your earning potential.

- ❏ Your knowledge of the local area and the country in general.

- ❏ Vehicle maintenance, reliability, and equipment. As soon as you are not available during the week due to a breakdown or for maintenance your earnings potential will obviously stop. Equipping yourself with the basics (eg check you have a legal spare tyre, a jack and brace, and a readycan etc) can make a huge difference, as can installing a GPS unit and some kind of internet access in your van. (See Deals and Discounts section of MTvan.com).

- ❏ Bad weather, illness and holidays. Hardy types who carry on working when the weather is foul and who take only a week or two holidays per year will make more money. Think about making and investment in tough and effective wet-weather and cold-weather clothing. A waterproof high-visibility jacket with a quilted lining, available from builders' merchants, may be a good idea.

© Tim Gilbert 2005

- ❏ Luck. It is impossible to overstate the effect which being in the right place at the right time can have on your income. If you get a really nice long job, and then another one comes in collecting nearby and going in the same direction, it's you're lucky day as you'll be being paid twice for at least some of the miles you're driving. Check with the courier company what their policy is on this, as some try to pay a lower rate for the second job.

- ❏ How well you play the system. When you are empty away from your home city you can increase your income by calling for a return trip from another courier company office, and by using TextMeMT (see MTvan.com) to alert other courier members that you are in their area. If you have internet access in your van, you can even bid for nearby collections from MTvan.com when you're empty miles from home.

- ❏ How busy your courier company is at anyone time. Every courier company has quiet days, weeks and even months, most noticeably in the summer. Developing relationships with many courier companies will help when it's quiet.

With all this in mind, you need to give yourself time. Four weeks is the absolute minimum that you should allow before you judge your initial success with any given courier company. Every day is different and you will find that some days go your way and on others you may wish that you had never got out of bed.

So it is better to look upon freelance courier work by the week, month or year rather than by the day, as things average out over time and you will get a more accurate picture.

Above all, don't be tempted to earn more by cramming in more deliveries than can realistically be done to their deadlines. If someone is paying you to deliver to a tight deadline, that deadline is all-important. Taking on and fitting in extra work that will make you miss that deadline is just foolish. You may make extra money that day, but you've thrown away your reputation, which will cost you more in the long run.

Of course, you'll often be handling valuable goods, and if you are careless, or even just unlucky, and a package is lost, damaged or stolen whilst in your care, you will not be paid for the job, and you may be charged for its replacement. So you should arrange your own Goods in Transit Insurance (see "Deals and Discounts" section of MTvan.com). Also advisable is Public Liability insurance, in case you injure someone or damage something while delivering.

As well as being valuable, the goods will usually be urgent, so if you break down, and cannot complete the delivery, and the courier company has to get another courier to complete the job, you may well not be paid your full agreed percentage. You may well even end up owing the courier company money, as you had agreed to undertake the delivery for an agreed price, and at your own risk. It's worth asking about the courier company's policy on this kind of thing at the outset.

It is an occupation that rewards hard work, self-discipline and a conscientious approach. If you're this kind of person, there's a good living to be made.

© Tim Gilbert 2005

Tony's Guide

to the courier industry

Tony's Guide

Here are some specific points in the form of a checklist:

☐ You'll need to equip yourself and your van. Your van should be either one of the many small diesel vans the size of a Ford Transit Connect, which will carry anything from an envelope to a pallet, or something much bigger like a high-top Sprinter. Which size you choose depends partly on your temperament (are you happy to load and drive something that big?) and partly about the demand in your area. If the choice doesn't seem obvious to you at the outset, start with something small and cheap, get to know your local market, and trade up if you think the money is there for running a bigger van.

☐ You will need an up to date street map of your local area and a UK road atlas.

☐ You should carry a few basic spares and bulbs with you and the tools to fit them.

☐ You will obviously need a mobile phone. Many customers and contracts require a proof of delivery immediately at the point of delivery, so you'll need lots of free minutes, and a bundle of texts for as little money as possible. We strongly recommend that you get yourself equipped to go on-line in the van, for which you'll need a suitable mobile phone with internet access. Make sure that it will access and display a full sized website like MTvan.com before you commit yourself. Some couriers take their laptop computer around with them, and use that for the internet. This may work for some people, but we recommend a "PDA" (a combined internet and phone arrangement). It's also possible to get satellite navigation systems to plug in to these phones, which can make the whole package very useful to you. This topic is covered regularly in the MTvan.com Forum, and there are links in the Deals and Discounts section of MTvan.com.

❑ You should have sufficient straps and bungee cords so that you can prevent packages from sliding around and getting damaged, and a few old blankets for providing extra wrapping and a buffer' between the consignment and anything else. It is your responsibility to ensure that the load is safely, securely and legally loaded, both during the loading process, and before driving away. A barrow may be a good idea, especially if you have a large van, as it'll save you time and backache while loading.

❑ You should always keep the load area of your van clean and dry to prevent damage to the stuff you're carrying.

❑ If you have to keep a package overnight, or over the weekend, for later delivery, you must obviously keep it safe from theft. This may even mean transferring the load to your house or garage. The load is your responsibility while it is in your care, and a loaded van is very attractive to passing thieves. You may find that the small print of your Goods in Transit insurance excludes cover for unattended loads, especially overnight.

❑ This should go without saying, but make sure you have a legal spare wheel, wheel brace and jack, the key to your locking wheel nuts, and membership of a recovery service. A spare ignition key is also useful, attached to a chain on your belt.

❏ You'll need money or credit cards (best of all one with Nectar Points or similar, as you'll be spending a lot) for fuel, lunch, tolls, and other expenses, and for emergencies.

Put simply, make sure that you have everything you need to do the job properly, and be organised so that nothing stops you earning the money when it's there.

Tony's Guide

"It takes 20 years to build a reputation and five minutes to ruin it. If you think about that, you'll do things differently." (Warren Buffet)

Tony's Guide
to the courier industry

This is perhaps the most important aspect of the job. The controller is the person in the courier company office who hands the work out to the couriers. Keep the controller aware of your progress so that he/she can in turn keep the customer aware. It will increase your earnings, as when there's a job nearby you'll have a better chance of being offered it.

If you are having difficulty locating a collection or delivery address — you have spent over 20 minutes searching to no avail, and you've asked at the local petrol station— let the controller know, and he/she will be able to advise the customer if necessary, and also assist you. You may find that the moment you say you're in trouble, he'll say "oh yes, everyone has trouble the first time finding that one – it's down the alleyway next to Woolworths". So let the controller know if you are running late for any reason.

© Tim Gilbert 2005

If you cannot complete a job for whatever reason — puncture, breakdown, incorrect address, kidnapped by aliens, accident, your first call should be to the controller.

Unless you're asked not to, call the controller with the "name and time" of the delivery as soon as you've done it.

Always contact the controller if you are doing a remote collection somewhere because during the time it has taken for you to make the first collection another pick-up in the same area may have come in.

Let the controller know if you are kept waiting anywhere, as it can be chargeable.

The more you keep in touch the more chance you'll have of being given "double-ups", ie work nearby going in a similar direction, and return journeys. You may spend £5 on phone calls in a week but then get a return or double up worth £50.

If you are doing a job for another courier company, let everyone know when and where you'll be empty.

In summary, the controller is trying to keep three sets of people happy; the customer, the courier, and the courier company owner. Do everything you can to help him keep everyone happy, and he will generally reward you with good work whenever he has it.

Getting proof of delivery (POD)   6

The actual "Proof of Delivery" is made up of three pieces of information:

- ❏ The actual signature.

- ❏ The printed name.

- ❏ The time signed for.

The "actual signature" is very rarely needed except if something goes to court, when you'll be pleased you got one, and that you kept the paper sheet.

The "printed name" and the "time signed for" are the two bits of information that you'll be asked for time and time again, so might as well pass them on to the controller (or enter them on MTvan.com if appropriate) as soon as you've received them.

This is just as important as keeping in touch with the controller. It is absolutely central to the service offered to the customer by the courier company - an immediate collection and delivery service with a guaranteed proof of delivery for every job. If you fail to get a POD for a job then the courier company is failing the customer.

Having said all that, there are certain circumstances in which it is simply not possible for you to get a POD. You may be delivering to a private address and arrive to find no one in, for example. Procedures vary between courier companies, so check with your controller, but generally courier companies insist that you contact their office for instructions before just posting the package (if small enough) or leaving it with a neighbour (if it's too large to post through the letterbox). Never assume that it's ok to act without specific instructions.

Now information on PODs in detail:

A full written POD sheet should include:

- ❑ full pick-up address;

- ❑ full delivery address;

- ❑ the person's signature;

- ❑ the person's name printed (it must be readable, as it's usually the name you'll be asked for, not the way the signature looks);

- ❑ the time at which the person signed.

- ❑ number of packages if more than one.

- ❑ waiting/loading time details.

The address details must include the sender's addresses, name, company name, street and town or postcode.

If just one of these elements is missing it is not a complete POD sheet, and you could find yourself being asked for information later that you can't provide.

In practice what often happens is that the person in receipt of the

Tony's Guide

to the courier industry

consignment will scribble something illegible on your sheet, possibly in the wrong place, and hand it back. The easiest way to resolve this is to ask their name (they may even have a name-badge) and print it for them along with the current time (use the 24 hour clock).

If they complete all parts of the POD, make sure to check that you can read their printed name and that the time is about right - its no use to you having all the info if it is unreadable or incorrect, and you only discover this when you're 50 miles down the road.

Most courier companies insist that you contact the controller if you cannot get a POD for any reason before handing over the consignment(s). If you have to do this, make a note of who at the courier company you spoke to and when, and exactly what they said.

As soon as you have the written POD you can text message it into MTvan.com if appropriate (see FAQ section on MTvan.com), or enter them in the "Give us a POD" section on the website.

POD sheets should be kept in a safe place, in an order that allows you to look them up quickly. File them, preferably at the end of each day or at the beginning of the next in the POD file in the courier company's office, or at your home or office, depending on local instructions.

The POD sheets are your only proof to the courier company's customer that the job has been done and therefore also your only guarantee of payment. Keep all your POD sheets for at least 12 months, giving the courier company time to request copy PODs from you, and for you to check your pay advice. However odd it may seem, don't be at all surprised to be asked to produce a POD sheet months after you've completed the job.

POD information is often required a week or so after you have delivered, and then again about two months later when the invoice is

© Tim Gilbert 2005

being queried by the customer.

It is sometimes tempting to think "I gave it to the nice lady who is always on reception, so that's ok", and not insisting on a proper signature, especially if you're busy, and especially if you deliver there regularly. But nice ladies on reception have a habit of turning into fire-breathing dragons when they are looking for someone else to blame for the loss of a mislaid parcel. So cover yourself every time; get a really good POD every time, and file it carefully.

Tony's Guide
to the courier industry

Always let the courier company's controller know as soon as possible if you are being kept waiting anywhere.

The customer is not usually charged for waiting until you have been waiting/loading for at least 15 minutes, to avoid lots of charges on their invoice for trivial amounts of time. If you are kept waiting for longer, then they are usually charged for that first 15 minutes and for each subsequent minute.

It helps the courier company's controllers plan for your next job, if you keep them informed of waiting time, and it also keeps the money right on the job.

If a job is pre-booked for a certain collection time and you happen to arrive early, the waiting time does not start until the pre-booked time has passed.

Customers do keep an eye on how long couriers wait in their reception and will, quite rightly refuse to pay the charges if they are incorrect.

It is your responsibility to make sure that the waiting time is actually added to the job on the computer by one of the office staff, it is not sufficient simply to report waiting time over the phone as it may be overlooked when the control room is busy.

You should note down on your POD sheet:

❑ full pick-up address;

❑ The length of time you were waiting and the times between which you were made to wait.

❑ Where the waiting occurred.

❑ The reason for the delay if known.

It's a good idea to make a note of all this on your POD sheet.

Generally the courier company cannot add waiting/loading time after the job has been invoiced, so it is up to you to let them know before this occurs, and best of all at the time.

It goes without saying that courier companies expect all couriers to behave reasonably and to take care in actually doing the job. Your actions, good or bad, will be seen as representative of the courier company as a whole and of course will be representative of their customer at the delivery point.

Behaviour

You should remain polite and helpful when dealing with customers at all times, even when under stress. For example, you might arrive at a customer's premises and they may think that you are late (you may be for one reason or another!) and a member of their staff may comment on this. The technique here is to apologise, and not to react badly to the comment. You can either ask them to take the matter up with the controller, or if there is a genuine reason for the delay (traffic congestion, foul weather, kept waiting at collection point, etc.) then feel free to tell them what kept you.

Here are some examples (real ones) of the kind of things not to say to customers as a reason for being late or in any other circumstance include:

"Well, I had to get the other two jobs on board first, mate!"

"Do you wanna have a go and see if you can do any better?"

"My van broke down on the way here but I think I've fixed it now."

"The other bloke they sent got lost/broke down so they sent me instead."

Always remember that you're the person on the spot, so you'll occasionally have to deal with some grief, but that ultimately it's up to the courier company to sort out any real or damaging disputes. That's what they're there for. Just make sure you don't add any fuel to the fire.

Taking care

By agreeing to carry out a delivery for a courier company, you have a serious duty of care to do the job with reasonable care in every respect.

Your vehicle has to be suitably equipped to undertake courier deliveries, and to take care of whatever you're carrying.

You have to take care of the package, and be sure that it is safe to be carried on/in your vehicle - safe, that is, for you, for on-lookers, for anyone helping you, and for the consignment, both during the loading and unloading process, and whilst on board during the journey.

If you do not think it is safe to take the job, call the controller. The judgement of whether it is safe for the consignment and/or safe for you, remains your responsibility.

Ensure that the consignment is suitable and suitably packaged for transit by your vehicle type, in the prevailing weather conditions if relevant.

This is particularly true for motorcycle couriers, who are often given a large piece of flat artwork only wrapped in brown paper, which is too large to fit into an artwork bag. It's usually very delicate, and must not be bent and is irreplaceable. To cap it all it is raining hard outside. The consignment is plainly not suitable to be transported by motorcycle, and an experienced motorcycle courier will politely inform the customer of this, and then inform the controller that a van is required for the job. Only a thoughtless beginner will strap it to his bike, get to the delivery point, and hand over a bent, soggy mass of paper which bears little resemblance to the item he was entrusted with at the outset. But it's been done.

An owner-driver courier in a van will often come up against the same kind of problems, and should take the same common sense attitude, to avoid any similar disasters.

Take every care that the consignment arrives at the delivery point in the same condition as was when you collected it.

It is worth making a written note of any flaws in the condition of the consignment (e.g. a crack in a mirror or piece of glass) before you leave the collection point (in these circumstances it would be the correct course of action to point out the flaw to whoever has given you the item(s), making a note of the person's name). If you're really well equipped, you could even take a picture of the damage using the camera in your mobile phone.

This way you are less likely to get blamed unjustly for damage done before your involvement with the consignment. To cover yourself further, alert the controller before accepting the consignment, and make a note of who you spoke to.

It's a good idea to carry polythene bags so that you can keep the worst of the weather off a package not made waterproof by a customer, and carry a blanket to help pack in the van.

All of this is common sense, of course, but a moment's carelessness with someone else's property can cost you and the courier company a lot of money.

In summary

To protect yourself and the courier company, check the following:

- ❏ That the consignment matches the description of the goods.

- ❏ That the goods are suitable for carriage in your vehicle.

- ❏ Whether handling assistance will be required either at collection or delivery point.

- ❏ Whether the goods are fragile and do they are suitably packed.

- ❏ Whether the goods are of a hazardous nature.

- ❏ That you have a sensible-looking delivery address.

- ❏ That you let the courier company know of any stops or delays.

- ❏ That while you have a consignment on board, you don't leave vehicle unattended, especially overnight.

- ❏ That common sense is being applied.

Tony's Guide

It is your responsibility to ensure that you observe the law at all times throughout the course of your work as a courier. If you're in doubt, you should contact a professional such as a lawyer or Citizen's Advice Bureau. You can also use the internet to make enquiries on the Government websites, such as www.dft.gov.uk.

Bookings you're offered should always have been accepted by the courier company from the customer with due consideration towards such things as:

- ❏ Timing schedules

- ❏ Vehicle capacities and capabilities

- ❏ Driver abilities

- ❏ Health and safety

- ❏ Dangerous/Hazardous Goods

It follows that the courier work should be offered to you, the courier, with the same considerations in mind. It is possible, however that an oversight or mistake may occur during the booking process which may only become apparent after you have arrived at the first collection point.

In a situation such as this you should ensure that all laws are observed at all times, and if unsure you must contact the controller before proceeding further. For example, if you think that the goods are dangerous, you should ask to see the courier company's risk assessment before accepting the job.

Vehicle and driving limits

It is your responsibility to maintain your vehicle, load the goods and keep them secure, and to drive within the rules of the road. Reputable courier companies will not generally encourage you to operate in such a way as to break the law. Obviously, if you feel you're being pushed into anything that does, you should discuss this with your controller. If you get no joy, you're always free to find work elsewhere, and you're probably better off doing so.

Hours of work

Most of the work that you do will take place at sometime between the hours of 0800 and 2200.

You should familiarise yourself with the drivers' hours regulations.

The current position is available on this unbelievably long link:

http://www.dft.gov.uk/stellent/groups/dft_freight/documents/page/dft _freight_504543.hcsp

The relevant section is reproduced here, but note that this may change, so do check the very latest situation for yourself, especially if any part of your journey is in Europe:

Part C - UK Domestic Drivers' Hours Rules

40. What are the UK domestic rules?

The UK domestic rules apply to most goods vehicles which are exempt from the EC rules.

41. What are the driving limits?

- Daily driving
  - ❑ A driver must not drive for more than 10 hours in a day.
  - ❑ The daily driving limit applies to time spent at the wheel, actually driving. Off-road driving for the purpose of agriculture, quarrying, forestry, building work or civil engineering counts as duty rather than driving time.

- Daily duty limit
  - ❑ A driver must not be on duty for more than 11 hours on any working day. A driver is exempt from the daily duty limit on any working day when he does not drive.
  - ❑ A driver who does not drive for more than 4 hours on each day of the week is exempt from the daily duty limit.

42. Are there any exemptions from UK domestic rules?

Yes, the rules do not apply to:

- drivers of vehicles used by the Armed Forces, the Police and

Fire Brigades;

- drivers who always drive off the public road system;

- private driving, ie not in connection with a job or in any way to earn a living.

Drivers of the following vehicles are exempt from the duty limit but not the driving limit:

- goods vehicles, including dual purpose vehicles, not exceeding a maximum permitted gross weight of 3.5 tonnes used:
  - ❑ by doctors, dentists, nurses, midwives and vets;
  - ❑ for any service of inspection, cleaning, maintenance, repair, installation or fitting;
  - ❑ by a commercial traveller;
  - ❑ by the AA, RAC or RSAC; or
  - ❑ for cinematograph or radio and television broadcasting.

43. What about emergencies?

The UK domestic rules are relaxed for events needing immediate action to avoid danger to life or health of people or animals; serious interruption of essential public services (gas, water, electricity or drainage), or of telecommunication and postal services, or in the use of roads, railways, ports, airports; or serious damage to property. In these cases the driving and duty limits are suspended for the duration of the emergency.

44. What about when travelling abroad?

The UK domestic rules apply only in the UK. But drivers must observe the national rules of the countries in which they travel. The Embassies of these countries will be able to assist in establishing the rules that might apply.

45. What records should I keep?

You must keep written records of your hours of work on a weekly record sheet. An example of such a sheet is at Annex D.

Operators are expected to check and sign each weekly record sheet.

Record books containing weekly record sheets are not available from The Stationery Office. The Vehicle and Operator Services Agency (see Annex E) can tell you the names of commercial printers who produce them.

NB. German national rules require drivers of goods vehicles between 2.8 and 3.5 tonnes to record details of their journeys in an AETR style logbook. This means that UK drivers have to use the logbook when they set out and whilst driving through the countries on journeys to or through Germany. Copies of these log books can be obtained from the Road Haulage Association (Tel 01932 841515),

46. Are there any exemptions from keeping records?

Yes, the following are exempt:

- Drivers of goods vehicles which do not require an operator's licence. This exemption does not apply to drivers of Crown vehicles which would have needed an 'O' Licence if the vehicle had not been Crown property.

- Drivers of goods vehicles on any day when they drive for 4 hours or less and keep within 50 kilometres of base.

- Drivers using an EC calibrated and sealed tachograph.

While courier companies are happy for you to work under these arrangements and to manage your own personal conditions, they should not encourage you to drive at any time if you are unfit. You should ensure that you take whatever breaks you feel are necessary to ensure that you are always fully awake and able to concentrate at all times.

When you stop for a break, make sure that you call the controller to keep him informed. Do not left your van and its load out of sight.

Mobile phones

The law is clear that you are not allowed to hold a mobile phone whilst driving, so you'll need a good hands-free kit or headset. Bluetooth headsets are very popular with couriers, and usually come free with mobile phones nowadays. Get a headset with the longest possible battery life.

Some stick-on Velcro to prevent your phone sliding all over the place in the van is a good idea, if you haven't got a proper hands-free cradle.

Lifting Injuries

Most of the work that courier companies offer you will be small items that are normally of a size that is comfortable for you to carry on your own. There may be an odd occasion that you are asked to deal with an item that is too big or heavy for you to carry. Once made aware of this, a courier company will usually make arrangements to give you some assistance. If there isn't assistance available on the spot, you should contact the controller.

Forklift trucks are only to be used by persons qualified, tested, and insured to use them, so don't be tempted to borrow one.

Making Yourself Available for Work   10

As an owner-driver courier, you are free to make yourself available at times to suit yourself. However, if your customer (the courier company) is relying on you to be available to enable him to service his customer, some kind of arrangement and commitment between you and the courier company will help everyone involved achieve their objectives.

On a general note it would benefit you to try and schedule your vehicle maintenance for the weekend regardless of where you work, or to have an alternative vehicle to use.

Tony's Guide

to the courier industry

Tony's Guide
to the courier industry

You should expect to be paid weekly, and at worst monthly by your courier company. If you're being asked to wait longer than that, you probably should look elsewhere for work, as it suggests that your money is at risk. If the courier company goes bust, you'll lose too much money.

It's also worth making a few discreet enquiries with the other couriers about whether there's ever been any problem with payments.

© Tim Gilbert 2005

Tony's Guide

to the courier industry

Keeping Records and Books   12

You should find yourself a local accountant, and take advice at the outset. This advice should cover all financial and legal aspects of your plan to become an owner-driver courier.

Your accountant is likely to recommend that you set up in business as a sole trader, but there may be sound tax reasons for setting up a limited company.

Your accountant will also advise you on the requirements for VAT, National Insurance, and Income Tax, and about the basic record keeping you'll need to do. You should also seek advice on the basics of invoicing and of "self billing", as it's an arrangement favoured by established courier companies.

You should also ask for advice about the rules governing your "self employed" status, as it's well worth avoiding breaking them.

Tony's Guide

Good Luck...

So far in this Guide, we've talked about how to make the most of becoming an owner-driver courier, with courier companies as your customers. There's a good living to be made if you approach it in the right way, and it has the advantage of being a relatively fun and risk-free enterprise, especially if you insure yourself properly.

The role played by courier companies involves shouldering some of that risk. The risk of not being paid, of paying out for damaged or lost parcels, of paying compensation for negligence etc, all fall mainly on the courier company. Taking on this risk, together with the workload of the invoicing and collecting the cash, is part of the value they add. This added value is reflected in the higher prices they charge their customer for your services.

If you're really sure you want to build from being an owner-driver courier to owning your own courier business, then read on...

Tony's Guide
to the courier industry

In the old days, and I mean before-fax-machines-came-along sort of old days, you could set up a courier company with just a pen, a reporter's notebook, an ashtray and a kettle for the couriers, an ex-BT transit van to do some of the deliveries in, and a typewriter for the invoicing. A few cards around local offices, and you'd soon be delivering urgent letters for local businesses.

How times have changed.

Since then, the same day courier industry has had to adapt to survive more changes than the Transit van has had facelifts.

Suddenly, email has replaced the courier for pretty much any correspondence that the fax machine hadn't already accounted for, and broadband is carrying graphical images which even isdn had been too narrow to handle.

These digital revolutions have reduced the industry to carrying "anything which can't be digitised", ie couriers are generally now carrying products, not documents.

The products that the new express pallet networks haven't poached, that is.

And nowadays customers won't stand for scruffiness of any kind, so there's been a revolution in the presentation of same day couriers and courier companies, with rule now being smart, well-turned-out couriers in smart vans, and imaginative courier company identities.

© Tim Gilbert 2005

Tony's Guide

Locally-owned and managed courier companies with a single control room now find themselves having to compete with large national and regional concerns with an office in every major town.

And 1000's of people have come into the industry, seeing it as an exciting way to earn money with their driving skills.

So what's the next big revolution?

Well as Bill Gates might say: "It's the internet, stoopid".

All same day courier companies, big and small, now compete for new business on the following issues, and those who embrace the benefits of the internet in the control room will be the winners by miles:

- ❑ **Be consistently excellent**

Customers now expect same day courier companies to smooth out the ups and downs of courier availability.

They want your Friday afternoon performance to be as perfect as your Monday performance. They want every part of the country to perform equally well, which is often a real management challenge for bigger same day companies who are only as good as the weakest office or depot in the group.

However big your operation, if you rely heavily on your "own fleet" of couriers, which is quick to shrink but much slower to grow when needed, your customer will always suffer worse service at busy periods, and is likely to try elsewhere.

Internet-based courier exchanges allow you to keep your own fleet to a sensible size for the amount of work you have, while still being able comfortably to cover all your work even at busy peaks.

Tony's Guide
to the courier industry

The various courier exchanges, such as www.MTvan.com and Courierline, between them have 1000's of members throughout the UK, the majority of them Owner Drivers, to give you your own virtually limitless "reserve fleet".

So the internet gives you access to many more couriers than you could ever have known in the past, in a much wider area, and more importantly, it allows you to manage their performance, without face to face contact.

And in recognition of the obvious anxiety many controllers feel about giving a job to someone they haven't met, there are "feedback" systems similar to the ones on eBay.

For maximum reassurance many internet-based couriers will even allow you to track their actual position, using positioning technology which tracks their mobile phone:

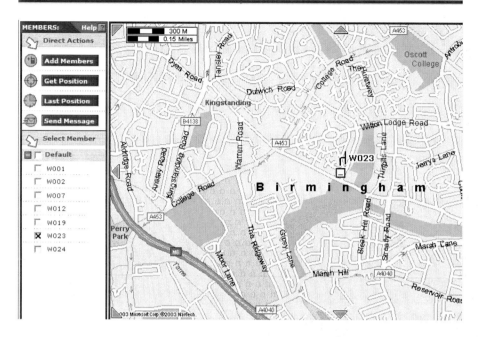

So nowadays the internet allows you to have a national fleet of couriers who you know you can trust and track just like your own fleet. And using the internet, you really don't have to suffer the cost of offices around the country to manage them.

❑ **Prove to your customer that he should stay with you**

Customers are now asking that you measure your performance, ie collection and delivery times, and measure them against pre-agreed Service Level Agreements.

You need to be offering POD data on-line or you're not even in the running.

The internet allows you to collect lots of detailed information like this, from couriers all around the country. Your couriers enter the POD data, and use that data to give your customers the overall performance summary.

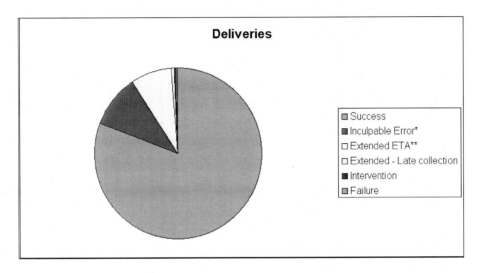

Deliveries

- Success
- Inculpable Error*
- Extended ETA**
- Extended - Late collection
- Intervention
- Failure

If your customers like your performance, they're less likely to look elsewhere. The internet allows you to prove to them that they like your performance.

❑ **Offer 100% national coverage**

Increasingly, you need national coverage, or you'll lose out to the big boys at tender stage.

Customers like to buy a range of products and business services from what they perceive to be national brands, whether it's stationery from Lyreco, overnight parcels from Amtrak, or cars from their nearest Ford dealer. They're buying from a local company with national presence. The same is true with same day courier, so increasingly, you need to look big and act big.

With such massive nationwide courier coverage on offer on the internet at the click of your mouse, you can nowadays be confident of being able to cover a job when you've "run out" of your own couriers, or if the job is collecting outside your usual area.

So one of the biggest barriers to courier company growth, getting the balance right between fleet size and the amount of work, is now a thing of the past, thanks to the internet.

❑ **Offer your customers more value**

You have a choice. You can be the courier company they choose because you're cheap, or the one they choose because you're more expensive but worth it.

The more basic you're offering, the cheaper you'll have to quote.

The more you offer your customer, the more you can charge, or at least the harder it is for him to look elsewhere.

The internet allows you to offer you customer more value, such as on-line booking, on-line POD enquiries, national coverage, and national performance measurement.

❑ **Charge competitive prices while making more profit**

If you're a medium sized courier company with, say, 25 couriers on the road, it's easy to be daunted by the power of the really big boys. With all that turnover, you'd expect them to be able to beat you every time.

But think about it. Their local office costs much the same as yours does, they employ the same number of people in the office as you do, and they can't make diesel any cheaper just by being big.

So locally they're no more profitable than you, and on top of that, they have the cost of the Head Offices and Area Supervisors and other regional management staff. How many "Regional Managers" and "National Operations Managers" do you employ at the moment? None, if you've got any sense.

So, you already have a clear head start over the big boys, in the way you are set up. Your costs are lower.

The internet allows you to maintain this advantage by covering work in a wider and wider geographical area without falling into the trap of wasting the extra money on more and more offices and staff to run it all.

By giving you access to couriers all over the country, the internet allows you to expand your business without the need for offices everywhere.

So if you get it right, you may well be able to win work from the big boys by offering very competitive prices against them, simply because your costs are lower.

And when a customer asks you "where are you based?", you can say "we're based on the internet, which gives us national coverage at great prices".

All of this is the reason why modern control rooms are now turning to the internet.

If nothing else, it you could save you a fortune in kettles and ashtrays.

Once you've made up your mind to build a courier business of your own, the first thing you're going to need is some customers of your own. Up to now, your customers have all been courier companies, middlemen, who have stood between you and some of the hard realities of finding and dealing with the "end user", the customer.

As you will have gathered, they play a useful role in getting the customers, taking on the work, sharing it out, paying you before they get paid, and generally taking on most of the risk. As an owner-driver courier, you will have benefited from all this, so you will have seen how much risk and work is involved. If you're sure you want to move out of the relative safety of being an owner-driver courier into the riskier world of becoming a courier company, start here.

The following sections will give you some ideas as to how to plan and carry out the sales campaign which you'll need to do to get some customers of your own. It's a formula.

Tony's Guide

to the courier industry

"Man who say it cannot be done should not interrupt man doing it." (Chinese Proverb)

Tony's Guide

to the courier industry

The sales potential of your area 14

The sales formula described in this section. It's cost effective and proven, but it's not easy. The essence of it is to identify the person who is responsible for deciding a firm's courier useage and making a promise to them about the quality of service you provide.

Then the salesman's promise is delivered is entirely in the hands of the operations team; the call taker, controller and courier. Or if you're on your own, your promise as the salesman has to be delivered by you as the courier. Many courier companies have started like this. It's a juggle, but it is possible. How this is done is covered in later chapters. Here we concern ourselves with one thing and that is how to get into the position where the promise can be made.

Tony's Guide

to the courier industry

Tony's Guide

to the courier industry

Getting sales leads

When approaching a new area in which you have not had a presence previously, start with mailshots.

There are two ways of doing this; postcard mailshots and letter mailshots.

Postcards are effective, because they attract more attention, but more time consuming. They must be addressed by hand, unless you can get hold of good address labels.

Don't be distracted by the need to get a database and a pc and labels; better to spend your time writing out a few hundred by hand.

Letter mailshots are useful but less effective, unless you have a contact name.

A simple way to get addresses is to walk round industrial and office estates and make a list of the likely looking companies there. You can even walk in to their reception area, and ask for the name of the person dealing with couriers. If it's the receptionist, make friends with him/her right there and then. Either way, get the name. A smile goes a long way.

Don't say you're new. Say you're local.

Make friends.

Tony's Guide

to the courier industry

Your postcard can say something simple like this:

\<your business name\> are a same day courier company offering *direct deliveries* locally and all over the country.

We have smart and professional couriers operating in \<your area\> and throughout the UK *right now*.

Friendly people, sensible prices.

For further *details call* **0xxx3 332200**

Name
Address

You can get these printed very cheaply using an on-line printer (see MTvan.com Deals and Discounts section). Put a simple logo, or black and white photo, on the front.

These postcards are a cheap way to:

- Establish the your business' brand name (If your target has not seen or heard of you already), and to introduce your logo as a recognised symbol in your area.

- Give the relevant phone number for enquiring or booking jobs on a card which can easily be attached to an office noticeboard.

The postcards should be targeted at companies likely to use your services (these are detailed later in the section **Target Markets**).

Here are three suggestions on distributing the postcards:

- Send off about 100 in one go by Royal Mail. Post them second class on a Tuesday, so they arrive towards the end of the working week, when demand for couriers is higher.

- Keep a file of who you have sent them to. Repeat to the same addresses one month later. This will jog the potential customer's memory and help create awareness of the presence of a your business operation in their area.

- You can then phone each one to try to get an appointment. Getting one is always easier when the target has heard of you. The postcards help with this. Don't say you're new; it's the last thing they want to hear.

The reason these cards work is simple. Eventually, almost everyone wants to change courier. This might be because they have fallen out with their existing supplier, or because their needs have changed, or because staff have changed, or one of many other reasons. You just have to be there for them, and be known to them and liked by them when this happens.

Tony's Guide

To achieve this, you have to phone them as well as sending them cards. Don't kid yourself; just posting out mailshots on its own doesn't achieve anything. So you have to phone them.

Phoning them means you have to be rejected 100's of times until you get one result. Eventually someone will say "You've called at just the right time, as we're looking to change our courier". No rejections, no result. So don't see rejection as a reason to stop phoning. Every rejection is one step closer to success.

You have some couriers working for you already, give the postcards to your couriers to distribute. If work is slack, it is easy to persuade couriers to do simple selling in between collecting and delivering. Explain the target markets to them and ask them to keep a record of any firms they visit who sound interested.

Hand them out yourself, either on your delivery rounds, or by just visiting local industrial estates and offices and "carding up", ie making sure that every receptionist has one of your cards.

Walking around your local industrial estates, handing out cards and making friends with people, is likely to be the single most effective use of your sales time.

If you're just starting out, you should strictly and carefully avoid directly targeting the customers of any courier business who currently gives you work. This kind of thing gets you a bad name, and will come back to bite you in the future. It's generally important that your competitors respect you, as customers often listen to what they say about you.

Tony's Guide

to the courier industry

Letter mailshots

17

This method is most effective when you have a contact name with a potential customer, i.e. when you have a sales lead.

Letters can be adapted according to what sort of customer you are aiming at, but here's an example. As you will see, it is a letter to send as a follow-up to a phone conversation. These are the most effective first contacts, but just sending letters out is pointless. It makes you feel like you're doing some sales, but without sales phone calls, sending letters rarely produces any results.

Technology Unlimited Limited
Technology House
Technology Avenue
Birmingham
B1 1AA

Attn James Geek

24th January 2004

Same Day Courier Requirement

Dear James

As discussed during our conversation today, I write to register our interest in tendering for your same day courier requirement when it comes up for renewal in April.

With our locally based office people and couriers, and our truly national coverage, I am confident that we can offer you not only a credible quality alternative to your current supplier, but a solution which adds value to, and cuts cost from, your substantial spend.

I can offer you excellent references from our other premium major customers, such as Example Ltd, Excellent plc, Satisfied & Co, and your immediate neighbours Nextdoor plc.

I would welcome an opportunity to meet face to face at any time, to discuss your requirements.

In the meantime, if ever your current supplier is ever even momentarily short of a van for you, please do feel free to call us.

Yours sincerely

Jim Keen
www.youramazingcouriers.co.uk

Following up with a phone call

18

As already mentioned, people never respond to the mailshot letter itself, but they may remember getting the letter or postcard if you call soon afterwards.

People who say "I've sent out loads of letters and heard nothing" just need to get on the phone and do the proper follow-up.

It is often easy to find out contact names by phone, to send the letters to. If you call a company and ask politely for the person in charge of purchasing courier services, you may not get a chance to actually speak to the buyer, but you will usually get their name. However, some receptionists are trained not to put through cold calls. In this situation, ask for the contact name so that you can send a brochure, as receptionists will usually give out a name for mailing information to. You can then send a letter, and call back the following day and hope to be put straight through, saying "I wrote to him yesterday".

The only way to sell is by speaking to the **MAN**:

Means (to pay you)

Authority (to give you the work)

Need (for what you are offering).

If the person you speak to lacks one of these you will not make a sale. It is worth remembering that a sale is not a sale until the invoice is paid, so always check that your potential customer looks as though he can pay his bills.

Call during the day, 1000hrs to 1200hrs and 1400hrs to 1600hrs are the best times.

Plan to do it, put it in your diary, prepare yourself to do it, sit down, clear your desk, turn your mobile phone and email off, close the door, and do it for the full two hours.

It's a numbers game, and you just have to put the time in. The more you time you spend phoning, the more likely you are to come across someone who wants to buy what you're trying to sell, ie who is looking for a courier company to use.

Once you have the contact name, it is worth trying to establish a relationship straight away. Ask:

- ❑ Who they are using at the moment.

- ❑ What service they require, ie what size vans, what they have delivered, what problems they are currently experiencing.

- ❑ Where The area covered by their requirement, and any regular delivery points

- ❑ When What times and how often they might need you, and when the current contract, if any, is up for renewal.

- ❑ Why they use couriers instead of overnights or vice-versa. You can point out that overnight parcels are priced by weight so it is often cheaper for to send pallets with you than by using an overnight carrier.

Use only open questions, never ask closed (yes/no) ones. If they don't answer straight away, never break the silence even if it is uncomfortable, they will eventually speak first and give away more than they wanted to.

Write everything down in a disciplined way.

When you have found out all you can about their courier requirement, tell them about how **FAB** you are:

- ❏ Features

- ❏ Advantages and

- ❏ Benefits,

making reference back to any problems or special needs they have.

While on the phone, always ask your prospects for referrals, ie who you else you can talk to, within their organisation. People will often recommend you to colleagues if they think you can solve their colleagues' needs. It also gives you credibility if you can say something like "Dave in Finance suggested I call you", especially if Dave is quite senior in the company.

Ask existing customers for referrals too, if people are happy with your service, they will be pleased to help you out.

Tony's Guide

Keep a diary so that when someone says to call back in a week, you don't forget. You can do this using Microsoft Outlook, or with a paper diary. Write down everything they say, so that next time you call them you can say things like "when we spoke last month you said you were thinking of reviewing your courier suppliers this month".

Set yourself targets of numbers of calls you will make each day and write down how many you actually do make to ensure that you have kept to the target. This is really important.

Always start each day's call with follow-up calls from your diary. Otherwise you'll waste many of leads you find, as you won't follow them up.

Eventually, everyone is looking for a courier company, so you need to keep in touch regularly. That way, you give yourself the best chance of calling just at the moment when they are reviewing their courier arrangements.

Once you've made the first call, if you get a "not interested at the moment" answer, put it back in the diary three months ahead, noting who you spoke to, and what they said, to be called again.

"Most sales are made at the sixth encounter.
Most salespeople give up after three rejections!"

Gil Carpel, Airborne Express

Writing sales letters is an art that can be mastered with practice. Here we highlight the four most common mistakes and offer some tips.

When anyone opens a letter or brochure, they think "What's in it for me?" Nothing else. So your first letter must convince them within the first few seconds that you can offer solutions to their problems. It takes only a few seconds after the envelope is opened for the judgement to be made: "read on or put it in the bin". So it's got to be right in the first few lines. Here is a list of common errors made by sales people, both in letters and face to face:

❑ **Error 1: Talking about yourself first**

Many sales letters begin with "I am...." and they continue throughout the whole letter to tell you about themselves and how terrific they are. You're your prospect wants to know is whether this courier business can seamlessly collect your package and deliver it before the deadline for a sensible price. Better to start "If your business has problems with its courier deliveries, we're here to solve them..."

❑ **Error 2: Giving irrelevant information**

A variation of the first, this usually involves stating the obvious in the first line, as in "The printing industry has tight margins, and nowadays you need to look after every penny". Unless it genuinely impresses and is relevant to their needs, it adds nothing to your credibility. Similarly a list of your equipment or vehicles with technical details means little. All people want is economic solutions to their problems. Better to say: "With many years of experience behind us, we think we know how to solve your delivery problems...."

❑ Error 3: Not understanding what is wanted

Most sales people don't listen properly. They concentrate on their sales pitch rather than listening to the prospect's problem and learning what he wants to buy. Always start by listening. If necessary, start by saying "I'd like to have an opportunity to listen to you, to find out about your use of couriers, and what your current problems are....".

People buy solutions and benefits, not services and features. You go to a mechanic not because he is a mechanic, but because he will fix your van. You choose a particular one because he is reliable, punctual, fair and easy to deal with, not because he's got more spanners than anyone else.

Nevertheless, you do need to back up your claims. So a good marketing document gives prospects a strong, credible indication of the range of problems you've met and solved, and the difference this has made to your customers. It helps reassure them that you will solve their problem and that it will be safe for them to deal with you. You're someone they can trust.

Take what you learn from listening to them to be people's real needs, and incorporate it into your sales letters.

❑ Error 4: Not showing how you will help

Look for and offer solutions, at every turn. List and highlight the problems you can solve. Technical detail is not necessary. For example, don't be tempted to say things like: "We use freelance subcontractors who get paid on an percentage basis, so they go as

Tony's Guide

fast as they can to do as much work as possible". They just don't want to hear it. They'd rather hear something like "You can call us any time day or night to book a delivery, and if your customer ever asks for a Proof of Delivery, it's all there on the website". You're offering to solve their problem of not being able to get hold of a courier company after office hours, and you're helping them answer their customer delivery queries.

Be brief, and remember that the main purposes of your letter is to be on their desk to remind them of you when they need to change courier, and to help them feel they've heard of you when they get your follow-up phone call.

Tony's Guide

"If A equals success, then the formula is: A = X + Y + Z, where X is work, Y is play, and Z is keep your mouth shut."

(Albert Einstein)

Finding out about the customer's needs

By whatever means you get to speak to your potential customer, there is certain information you would like from them. It may not always be possible to find all of these out:

- ❏ Customer Name & Address in full

- ❏ Postcode

- ❏ Contact names and positions of decision makers

- ❏ Phone numbers and email address

- ❏ The nature of their business

- ❏ Their current courier supplier

- ❏ How often they use couriers

- ❏ When they are planning to review their courier arrangements.

It is also very important to find out what they want from their supplier. It is important to listen rather than ask here. They are likely to tell you what is wrong with their existing supplier as well as specifying exactly what it is they want. If they don't tell you, invite them to. "Are you experiencing any particular difficulty with your current supplier?" They then list what's going wrong. You listen. Turn their list of problems into a list of solutions you can provide. Then you sell them the idea that you can solve those problems for them.

Key points to be clear on are:

- ❑ The response times they require, how long they tolerate between booking the job and the courier making a collection

- ❑ The services they will require: local / regional / long distance / national coverage for collections / contract run / UK / international / overnight / out of hours / logistics storage / motorbikes / small vans / transit vans / larger vans

- ❑ Any reporting or specific accounting requirements they have for example: one job per invoice / jobs in numerical order of reference on invoice / separate accounts for different departments / Proof of Delivery summary reports

Write down any other details you discover. All information is useful. Make notes in the meeting or on the phone, then later use Excel, or Access, or a Contact Manager system to record all of this, or use paper contact forms, or a diary. If they're completely happy, make a note to call them again in three months time.

Tony's Guide

to the courier industry

"Success is going from failure to failure without a loss of enthusiasm." (Sir Winston Churchill)

Tony's Guide

to the courier industry

Having found the name of the person who will have the authority to make the buying decision, and assessed the courier needs of his/her company, there are various pieces of written information that you may want to send them. These may include:

❑ A map showing the location of your courier business, if it's nice and local, as often this is important in the mind of the buyer. You could use something like streetmap.co.uk.

❑ An account application form for them to fill in, which also shows your terms and conditions

❑ A Mission Statement if you have one

❑ A single sheet of A4 listing the benefits of choosing you

❑ A simple letter acknowledging the fact that you've spoken on the phone

❑ A price list, showing your minimums, your prices per mile, and some examples.

Tony's Guide

to the courier industry

Sending a brochure

The best format for your brochure is likely to be a loose-leaf folder, so you can vary the content according to who you are sending it to. You will need to use your judgement about which pages the potential customer is likely to find interesting. Don't put everything in for no reason. Keep the folder uncluttered and to the point. It is often worth including a letter to the potential customer outlining how exactly we can meet his requirements. You can buy a neat clear plastic folder from a stationers to put it all in. You can buy simple stickers, from on-line printers, to personalise them. Post it, or if very local, deliver it very quickly with a smile.

Emailing a brochure

Having the information ready to email immediately to the person you are speaking to is very effective, and the preferred means of receiving sales material for many people now. Ensure that it leaves your pc virus-free. (There's a free virus checker on the Deals and Discounts section of MTvan.com).

Faxing a brochure

Even whilst you are on the phone talking to the purchaser, you can fax them the information.

Ask the purchaser for his fax number, and fax him any relevant material you have, including an account application form), and ask him to fill in the application form and fax it straight back.

Website brochure

Get yourself a website for use as an on-line brochure. MTvan.com can create one for you, for a modest fee. Sometimes people like to look at your website while speaking to you on the phone. It helps them decide whether to invite you for an appointment.

Your website should be clean and uncluttered, with a brief summary about what makes you special, a list of the kind of customers you currently work for, your contact details, and a contact form. You website should also allow your customer to book and enquire on their bookings. MTvan.com can provide you with a page to do this, to include in your website.

Websites allow people to judge, and usually reject, you at first sight, so be very careful about what you put on the internet in the name of your company.

In Summary

Above all, remember that people you are talking to are generally busy, so you have to make it easy for them to hear about you, to remember you, to choose you, to contact you, and really easy for them to start using you, in amongst all the other things they are trying to deal with.

So you need to follow up with a simple phone call, the purpose of which is to say "So when would you like to start using us?"

Tony's Guide

to the courier industry

"If you think you can, you can. And if you think you can't, you're right". (Henry Ford).

Tony's Guide

to the courier industry

Tony's Guide
to the courier industry

For many companies, especially smaller ones, filling in your application form and trying your service may be enough to get them hooked and trying you out.

Once your new customer has faxed you a completed account application form, and you have checked that the collection address is the same as that on the form, you are in a position to start working for them on account.

If you'd rather they paid by credit card, MTvan.com can help you with this if you don't have a merchant account.

Some larger customers who are planning on spending a great deal on courier services are likely to want to meet you before they decide to leave their current supplier. For these customers there is more of a commercial risk for them associated with leaving their existing supplier. This risk is usually in the area of disruption to their business, distraction caused by managing the change, delivery errors happening while new couriers get to know the delivery addresses, that the prices you quote will somehow turn out to be higher in some way, and so on. These are "buyer's anxieties" which you have to overcome, having first found out what they are.

Try to make appointments for customers' slack times, and if possible group the visits together geographically, to reduce your travelling costs. If it's a really big prospect, you may want to take a laptop with you and make a presentation using Microsoft PowerPoint. Only do this once you're really good at it, so practise on someone who you can really trust to tell you if you're rubbish. Otherwise it's better to

Tony's Guide
to the courier industry

"just go round to discuss your courier requirements". Be there to listen, and to solve their problems, not to get them to listen to how wonderful you are.

"I owe my success to having listened respectfully to the very best advice, and then going away and doing the exact opposite". (G. K. Chesterton)

Marketing

You need to be very clear about what marketing is.

Marketing is deciding upon, and communicating "the whole idea of your business". What your service is, at what price, when it's available, how people should actually buy from it, what colours it uses, the name, the pricing, its location and coverage, and so on.

When you've decided on these and similar elements, it adds up to your "market positioning".

This section deals with the market positioning of your business.

Positioning matches the features, characteristics and benefits of your service with the wants and needs of people, your customers. Once you've worked out the details of your positioning, you need to communicate it to the people you're aiming at.

Marketing is not selling. Selling is simply a means of helping a potential customer to reach a decision to buy. This only happens when the customer and the service have been properly matched.

To make the marketing work, the service and the potential customer must be brought together at the same time, in the same place and with the same interest. Then you want the customer to make a decision on the basis of what he perceives you as offering compared with what your competitors have on offer. He chooses the one that suits his own preferences, regardless of quality, and in his own mind will be juggling with a whole spectrum of variables such as price, design, performance, habit, prejudice, fashion, value and personal relationships. The bottom line is that he/she will come up with a simple conclusion that "I like it" or "I don't like it", and if it is the latter he/she will go away and buy whatever it is he/she "likes better" from somebody else.

The crunch question is "What is the customer looking for?" and your success in marketing lies in getting it more nearly right than your competitors. If you get it right you make money. The customer therefore has the power of life or death over your business.

The whole purpose of your business is to generate sufficient income to achieve your stated objectives, and income comes solely from satisfying customers. Every single function in your business should be focused on that one objective.

Tony's Guide

Question Yourself:

Make sure you know the answers to:

- ❑ "Give me a really good reason why anyone should actually buy it from you rather than from somewhere else"

- ❑ What is so special or different about your service that they should choose to spend their money with you"

- ❑ Is there anything unique about your quality, features, specification, service, design, convenience, availability, presentation, or performance that actually matters to the customer?

- ❑ Which customers don't you want?

- ❑ Which customers do you want?

- ❑ Where are they and how many of them are there?

- ❑ How do they go about making their buying decisions?

- ❑ What actual benefits will they get, and would they get more benefit from buying something else.

You really must know the answers to all of these, and rehearse them.

❏ Action required:

Make sure you know who your target market is. See the next section for this. Look at what your competitors are offering and make sure you know why your business services more closely correspond to what they actually do want, or what they actually will want in the future.

You can find this out by phoning them and asking them, usually, and by looking at their website. Work out areas in which you offer a better service or are better value than they are.

From all of this, decide on price, presentation, service quality and selling method, and keep this clear in your mind.

Respond to changes in the market, such as the arrival or disappearance of a competitor, or changes in their prices or service. If you fail to supply what your customers really do want they will simply take their money and spend it with someone who does.

In the end, business is about people, it is about understanding what they want, about supplying it when they require, wherever, whenever, and however they want, at a price they are prepared to pay that maintains your margin.

Tony's Guide

to the courier industry

"One important key to success is self-confidence. An important key to self-confidence is preparation."

(Arthur Ashe)

Tony's Guide

to the courier industry

Create a strong corporate image which identifies you for what you are; a well presented, efficiently run, professional and helpful courier service. Be consistent in everything the customer encounters so that everything they hear, see, feel, taste or smell tells them that you understand what they want and that we have it. People tend to buy with their emotions, not their minds. Your business appeals to them on that level.

There's often no need to spend money on a designer. You can, for example choose a name that allows you to use some commonly and freely available images as your logo, such as an @ sign like this:

@ Couriers

Quality couriers @ your service @ a moment's notice

Or a plus sign like this:

courierplus+

= quality couriers + top service + great prices +++

www.courierplus.co.uk

Be careful, though, as you'll need a website, and some characters (like @) can't be used as part of a website domain name.

You can check on domain name availability using websites like www.UK2.net.

You should search on www.google.co.uk, and on www.companieshouse.gov.uk, for the name you are proposing to use, and check your local Yellow Pages.

Tony's Guide

"You don't get a second chance to make a first impression." -
ANON

Tony's Guide

to the courier industry

Pricing

People often ask: "What should I charge?"

The main thing which influences this, is what everyone else in your area is charging. There'll be a range, and you have to find your place in that range.

It's important that people feel they can get what they really want at a price they regard as fair. Don't undersell yourself, and don't try to be the cheapest, as most people know that if something is cheap it's likely to be disappointing. You have to let them know it's not the cheapest, but that it is good value for what they are getting.

The price is an important part of your image and will tell people a lot about you, so long as it is consistent with and does not contradict the remainder of your perceived image. It has to be roughly in line with what your competitors are charging, so you'll need to know their pricing in detail. You can do this by asking them (just phone them up) or by asking their customers, or by looking at their website. You'll be surprised how easily this information is obtainable.

Tony's Guide

People often make two mistakes about prices.

- ❏ One is that they think they have to be the cheapest to get the work. This is not true. Some buyers actually reject the cheapest, on the basis that the cheapest is likely to be the lowest quality. Generally, customers who choose a courier company solely on the basis of lowest price, are the customers you want your competitor to have.

- ❏ The second common mistake is to assume you have to make a great secret of your prices, and hide them from your competitors. Following on from the first mistake, this is not necessarily the case. Just because your competitor knows your prices it doesn't follow that he'll be able to take the work from you. Your customer chooses you, and stays with you for a variety of reasons, one of which (usually) is that your prices are not higher than he is comfortable with. As long as you are looking after your customer, and your prices are not extreme, you don't need to worry too much about keeping them secret.

In 2005, prices outside London range from 75p per loaded mile, to £1.10 per loaded mile for a small van, depending on region, so you will have to do some research in your area.

This topic is covered frequently in the Forum on MTvan.com.

Tony's Guide

to the courier industry

"Without a positive mental outlook, you have nothing"

(SVEN GORAN ERIKSSON)

Tony's Guide

to the courier industry

Promotion and advertising   27

People will not buy your courier services unless they know they exist, and how they can get them. They also need to know that somebody (you) has taken the trouble to understand exactly what sort of courier service they want, and that you'll provide it at a price they regard as being attractive in relation to the demand that is being satisfied.

It is all about communication. Providing the service isn't enough; people need to know that you provide it, and that it matches their needs.

Yellow pages is a good place to start. Try to find out how other courier and similar businesses in your area get new business enquiries. Yellow Pages ads work brilliantly in some areas, but are ignored in others. Radio advertising (either of your courier service, or to recruit for staff and or couriers) is a very good way of advertising your business locally in a non-threatening way, but it can be very expensive.

Cheaper than that to start with, is joining all the "business networks" in your area. Check out what Business Link and your local Chamber of Commerce offer in your area. Check out **www.businesslink.gov.uk**.

You'll meet lots of local business people at their breakfast events. It's a great way of turning yourself from being a stranger to being someone these people know and trust enough to try using for their courier work.

If you are any good at public speaking, you could offer to give one of the talks. If not, at least ensure that you ask an intelligent and friendly question at the end of everyone else's talk. It gives you an opportunity to raise your profile locally: "Hi, everyone, my name is John Smith from Courierplus.co.uk, and the question I'd like to ask is…"

Do-It-Yourself Public Relations is also worth some effort. PR isn't just about sending out press releases, though this is a start. You have to create news for the purpose of providing content for your press releases.

News is easy to create. Sign up a new customer. (FABcouriers sign up ABC plc for local deliveries). Take on lots of couriers (FABcouriers creates three jobs locally). Recruit someone (FABcouriers take on new customer services manager). Win or enter a competition (FABcouriers runners up in "Best local company" competition).

Set yourself a target of the number of press releases you want to send out every month, and make the time to do it.

❑ Selling:

"Selling" is getting people to make a decision to buy, and then hand over their money in return for your solution to their problem. Decide who is going to do the seeling, where, when and how? Does your salesman have the necessary people skills to handle a direct person to person encounter? If your salesman is you, do you have the skills? If you don't, get some training, get some practise, and ask yourself the question again.

❑ Access to the service:

Most work booked with your courier business is booked by telephone. There should be people available to take bookings 24 hours a day, 365 days a year. It is vital that you have enough people to take the bookings at any one time, or a system of diverts for the overload calls. Increasingly nowadays, people like to book business services on the internet. If you're being asked for this, you can now set it up quite easily using a booking web page provided discreetly by MTvan.com.

❏ **Service:**

This is part of the total package on which people base their decisions. What extra value will they hope they're being offered before, during and after the sale and to what extent will this influence their decisions? Learn the key issues in your market.

❏ **Monitoring and Control:**

Having a formal system for getting feedback from the people you are trying to satisfy so that you can adjust to their needs, wants and desires, is important. Your business should always use customer satisfaction questionnaires, enclosed with your invoices.

They're a brilliant way of getting testimonials and references for you to use in your sales effort. All you do is send out letters with your invoices, asking for feedback "for quality audit purposes". Lots of people will write back, and you can use their letters as references.

It is important that you know what customers actually want. Quite simply, you remain in business this way.

Tony's Guide

"Don't assume your customer is as happy as you are. Monitor customer reaction on an on-going basis"
- JACK WELCH (ex CEO, General Electric).

Tony's Guide
to the courier industry

In summary, your marketing plan is the method you choose to bring your service and your potential customers together. It will include:

- ❑ How your drivers appear

- ❑ How their vans will look

- ❑ How you answer the phones

- ❑ How smart you keep your office

- ❑ How you present yourself on paper and on the internet

- ❑ What level your prices are set at.

Tony's Guide

to the courier industry

"Its funny but the more I practice the luckier I get."

(GARY PLAYER)

SWOT

28

It's worth taking a bit of time on a regular basis (at least every three months) to work out and write down the Strengths, Weaknesses, Opportunities, Threats, and Constraints which affect your business.

Once you have them listed, you can work out a plan to build on and exploit your strengths, and to reduce your exposure to your weaknesses. Keep an open mind for opportunities, and decide whether to dodge or defend yourself from immediate or long term threats. Watch out for constraints; analyse them carefully them and plan around them. Here are some common examples; some of them are linked:

- ❏ S: Your courier business has a solid reputation for customer service.
- ❏ S: Your courier business pays a very low rent, so costs are low.
- ❏ W: Your courier business is indistinguishable from all the others locally
- ❏ W: Your courier business is very slow to invoice and collect cash
- ❏ O: An industrial estate is being built next door
- ❏ O: Your biggest competitor has become lazy and complacent
- ❏ T: Your biggest customer accounts for a majority of your sales
- ❏ T: A national courier company has opened a branch in town
- ❏ C: You are always short of cash
- ❏ C: You only have two vans.

Tony's Guide

to the courier industry

Your target markets

29

There are many ways of getting hold of lists of potential customers for various different areas, and of course, the customer types for different areas will not always be the same. You need to decide first where the work is, and what the limits of your sales area will be.

This is dependent on how far you mind travelling to see a potential customer, and on how wide your coverage is when it comes to being able to collect quickly. If you're relying purely on your own local regular freelance couriers to collect, you'll be limited to customers located within your home town or city.

Increasingly courier companies can now manage perfectly well to get customers throughout the UK, using a network of couriers and courier companies located wherever their customers are. This is the principle behind MTvan.com.

Here is a list of the various types of businesses and organisations which tend to require same day courier services.

© Tim Gilbert 2005

Tony's Guide

- ❏ Banking, Finance, Insurance, Accountancy

- ❏ Distribution

- ❏ Manufacturing

- ❏ Publishing and printing

- ❏ Machine parts especially where production lines waiting are expensive.

- ❏ Engineering / automotive

- ❏ Printing, bookbinding and paper goods

- ❏ Design and print.

Tony's Guide
to the courier industry

Your salesperson may well be you to start with, even if you are the kind of person who normally says "I'm not a salesman".

If you're going to make a success of your business, that is going to have to change.

Selling is about managing the moment of decision. It is the end point of your entire business and marketing strategy. It is the only aspect of your business that increases the prosperity of your courier business. It is about creating the moment when your prospect says "Yes" or "No" to your proposal.

It's mainly about people; identifying their wants, needs, desires and motivations and satisfying them profitably. It's about communication between buyer and seller and the identification of common interests, and it's about knowing exactly what you are trying to achieve and planning how you are going to achieve it.

To be a successful salesperson, you have to go out and find out what the customers can use from the courier services you are able to supply and ensure they buy it from you.

If you are doing all this yourself, you'll have to be really disciplined, especially if you're running the business as well.

If you are managing a salesperson, you have to delegate effectively. Here are some guidelines on successful delegation:

© Tim Gilbert 2005

- ❏ Communicate the task: "Sell this kind of courier service to these people at this price by this means using these tools"

- ❏ Set the task in context: "We're running a growing courier business here, and you're key to our growth".

- ❏ Communicate the standard you expect: "You're here to make at least 75 cold call phone calls a day for 2 days a week, resulting in 3 appointments a day for 3 days a week, to open 10 new customers every month, spending at least £100 per week"

- ❏ Give clear authority: "As long as you're selling according to the rules laid down, you have full authority to open new accounts spending up to £200 per week, and above that I want to sign off the prices your are offering.

- ❏ Provide support: "Full training will be given for the first month, and any time you need help or advice with anything unusual, I'm here for you".

- ❏ Get buy in: "Tell me now if any of this doesn't work for you".

A sale is a business transaction that ticks six boxes:

- ❑ an order has been placed;

- ❑ the service has been carried out;

- ❑ it has been paid for;

- ❑ the service has been analysed;

- ❑ it has been found to be satisfactory;

- ❑ this satisfactory outcome has been reported to the customer.

There are two main reasons why your sales effort may not work:

The marketing strategy is not valid.

You are talking to the wrong people about the wrong things, at the wrong time, in the wrong way, or you are not doing enough of it.

The final link (ie actually doing the job) is weak.

Many courier companies invest substantial sums in equipment, advertising and promotion, marketing, selling etc, but are weak at the last crucial link in the chain. When that phone rings, will you be able to cover the work? This has for years been one of the real limiting factors in a courier company's growth, as it's too expensive to keep vans available just in case demand increases.

Tony's Guide

Nowadays you can use MTvan.com to cover your excess demand. You just invite bids when you're running out of options with your own vans.

"Nothing is particularly hard if you divide it into small jobs"
- HENRY FORD

Tony's Guide
to the courier industry

Quite often there is a time lag between starting your sales campaign and beginning to see some result. So you have to keep your nerve for a while. If things aren't working after a sensible amount of time, you could review the situation along the following lines:

- ❑ Check that the marketing is right

- ❑ Do more selling

- ❑ Do better selling

- ❑ Check that the right people are doing the selling

- ❑ Manage them properly

- ❑ Check that you will be able to cope with the demand when it starts working.

- ❑ Keep your nerve.

© Tim Gilbert 2005

Selling time will be employed more profitably if you know you are talking to someone who:

- ❑ Has a real need for what you are selling.

- ❑ Can see a significant difference between what you are offering and what your competitors are offering which matters to him.

- ❑ Has the means of paying for it.

- ❑ Has the authority to make the buying decision.

- ❑ Can believe what you are telling him.

- ❑ Can access your courier service as and when he needs it.

This will happen if your research and marketing strategy have been carried out correctly. The result will be that you will be selling to carefully targeted individuals where there is a high level of probability that you should be able to make a sale. You will know what you are trying to sell, how you intend to sell it and why the customer should buy it. In this way you can avoid wasting valuable selling time.

Here's a diagram to illustrate what you should be selling, and what you should not be selling:

Tony's Guide

to the courier industry

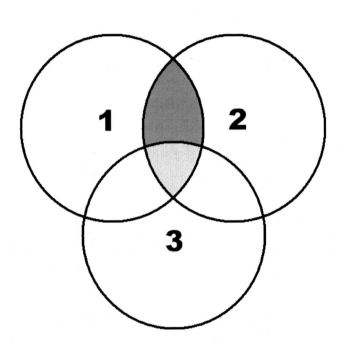

Key:
1 = what your company can do.
2 = what your customer wants.
3 = what your competitor can do.

Your own courier company's competitive advantage lies in the dark grey area.

You can sell what your customer wants and what only you can supply.

Head to head competition with your competitors (light grey in the middle) is more time consuming and difficult.

Stick to the dark grey area if possible. To do this, you need to be very clear where the dark grey area is in your business. You need to be clear what it is, and you need to work to strengthen it, and to tell the world and your team about it at every opportunity.

It is pointless trying to sell something which you can't supply or which your customer doesn't want. It is difficult, but not impossible to sell when a competitor has a clear advantage or is equal with you.

In the end, customers will only do what they want to do, what they need to do and what they are able to do. They will not buy unless they can afford it, have the authority to make the decision and are motivated to want what you are offering. Selling is therefore about exploring and understanding another person's motivations, likes, dislikes, preferences, prejudices, needs, desires, aspirations and individual circumstances. And then matching them precisely with the package you have on offer. This means thorough research and careful planning and preparation, and a detailed knowledge of the service, the customer, the competition and your market.

Above all, don't be put off by rejection.

Tony's Guide

Get the marketing right: Sell the right thing to the right person.

Do more of it: Spend more time listening to and talking to prospects.

Do it better: Squeeze more out of the time with each prospect, and above all learn to close the sale. "Your account is open; when are you planning to book your first job with us?"

Manage the process: It will not happen on its own; you have to make it happen through careful analysis and meticulous planning backed by personal discipline. This means calling again and again, and overcoming all objections, until you close the sale.

Tony's Guide

"If you don't sell, it's not the product that's wrong, it's you."
- ESTEE LAUDER

Taking on couriers to cover the work

Once you've got some customers, you'll need some couriers.

Before you've got some couriers, you'll probably be the courier as well as the salesperson. This is quite normal. In fact it's a great way of finding out who is spending money on couriers. For every collection you make from your customer, there's a delivery to a prospect. Make sure you collect contact names as you go along, and use them in your sales efforts later:

"We do a lot of work for ABC Ltd who I believe you do quite a lot of business with, and I'm keen to make an appointment with you to discuss helping you solve any delivery problems you may have".

In addition to relying on your own efforts as a courier, you can use MTvan.com to invite bids on the courier work you can't cover yourself.

If your sales effort is going well, you may soon also want some regular couriers to help you out with the deliveries.

You may be able to form an alliance with one or more local owner-drivers, agreeing to "swap work" in return for sensible prices, and an agreement not to poach customers from each other. This is increasingly the next step for many people who are making the transition from owner-driver to small courier business. You can look for these alliances amongst the Members on MTvan.com.

If you have a really steady flow of work, you may well soon want "couriers of your own" to call on, in a more formal relationship.

© Tim Gilbert 2005

Tony's Guide

The importance of choosing the right people effectively to represent your business at the "sharp end" of your same day courier operations in the U.K and abroad cannot be overstated.

The actions, conduct and competence of each of your couriers will be seen to be representative of your company as a whole and so it is obviously very important to take great care at the interview stage to only choose those candidates who will be an asset to your business. If you are in doubt it is better to be cautious.

Similar care must be taken in the training process, as new couriers, however willing, can only meet your high standards if they are properly trained in your way of working.

Tony's Guide

"Entrepreneurs are simply those who understand that there is little difference between obstacle and opportunity and are able to turn both to their advantage."
 - VICTOR KIAM

Tony's Guide

to the courier industry

Tony's Guide
to the courier industry

Placing classified advertisements in national newspapers, such as The Daily Mirror, and in local papers can be effective, if expensive, ways of attracting couriers. There are a few trade magazines, such as Courier Direct Magazine.

Alternatives include contacting your local Jobcentre or placing cards in local newsagents or at adult education colleges. You can also use MTvan.com to place recruitment notices on the Forum.

When you get some enquiries, there are a few simple points you can make to ensure that both you and the caller are not wasting each other's time:

❑ All your couriers are freelance subcontractors responsible for their own income tax and national insurance contributions, ie this isn't a job, and therefore it isn't Pay As You Earn.

❑ Your couriers provide their own vehicles - vans (if you do not allow cars) must be white, not more than 5 years old.

❑ Prospective couriers must be able to provide full and current driving related documents for your inspection, including "courier" or "business" cover on their insurance, and good evidence of identity and home address.

Having covered these points, if the caller is still keen the next step is to take down their contact details.

Having invested to get these contacts it is important to keep a record of names, phone numbers and vehicles. Contacts lists are always useful in future emergencies.

"Small opportunities are often the beginning of great enterprises". (Demosthenes)

Tony's Guide

Interviewing couriers

The main purpose of the interview is to get a feel for the character of the person, and to get a feel for their general appearance and manner.

Before proceeding further it is a good idea to have a look at their vehicle, as there is obviously no point going further if this is not suitable.

Begin the interview by asking them to tell you about their history, finding out what courier work they have done in the past. How they enjoyed them, how long they did them for and particularly the reasons they moved on to other things should reveal something of the person's attitudes to work in general. If the interviewee reveals a list of disputes and dissatisfactions which caused each job change then he/she may well soon get fed up with life as a courier with you too - and what you want to avoid is making the considerable effort involved in training the new person only to have them leave within a few weeks.

Any past experience in the courier industry or a similar field can be both good and bad news. On the up side, the person should have a good geographical knowledge and a reasonable idea of what the job entails. On the downside, the person may have picked up bad habits which he/she may cling to and which might cause problems. You will need to ask plenty of questions so that you can decide whether the person is receptive to and liable to be happily co-operative with your way of working. People with no relevant experience can sometimes be a better choice as they accept direction and advice more readily.

© Tim Gilbert 2005

Listen to your instincts, as well as being methodical.

If things are looking likely, a couple of points to get across are:

You are an expanding national courier brand established in [year] with over [numbers] couriers around the country - so they will be joining a successful growing company.

In order to maintain this growth, to stay ahead of the game, you have to move with the times - constantly assessing and when and where necessary completely re-working your operating procedures and marketing outlook, - to meet the new challenges of the marketplace and provide consistently the highest standards of service possible within the industry. What this means to your couriers is that you expect correspondingly high standards of behaviour from them along with the willingness and flexibility adapt to the new challenges with you. People who routinely resist new ideas and approaches to things you will probably not be happy working with you.

Here are a few examples of what you should make it clear you are looking for:

- [ ] Getting a full POD (signature and legible print) and time on every single job, without exception, no POD = no pay.

- [ ] Being available for work as agreed.

- [ ] Being generally happy and willing to do each job which comes along whether local or long distance unless there is a sensible reason why you cannot.

- [ ] Honesty, integrity, courtesy and conscientiousness - you expect your couriers to behave reasonably and take care whilst actually doing the job, as their actions will be viewed as being representative of your business as a whole.

You can say that in your opinion earnings potential is excellent but ultimately the main factor governing earnings is people's aptitude for the job and how hard they are prepared to work - it is very important to emphasise this point to ensure that people realise that considerable effort and ability are required to make a go of it.

You can even show them examples of some of your current couriers weekly earnings in order to illustrate your point - show your hardest working and least hard working couriers weekly earnings.

Earnings may be low initially during the period when a new courier is familiarising himself with the locations of your customers and the requirements of the job itself and so you should suggest that they should give it at least four weeks before deciding whether to stay or not.

Working as an owner-driver courier is found by many to be a rewarding, stable, refreshingly "different" way of making a living which appeals particularly to the hardworking, independent, self-disciplined type of person with lots of common sense.

Having made these points you could ask them if there is anything which has not been covered to their satisfaction by what you have said so far. Expect, and have answers to the following:

- ❑ "What is the least I will get paid for an individual job?"

- ❑ "How many of these minimum rate jobs will I be doing in a week?"

- ❑ "How much long-distance work am I likely to get?"

- ❑ "Do you guarantee your couriers a minimum level of earnings?"

- ❑ "Will I get treated the same as your other people if I join you, or do you favour long-serving couriers?"

Tony's Guide
to the courier industry

Summary:

When speaking to people either on the phone or face-to-face you should emphasise the positive aspects of being a courier but do not gloss over the fact that it is hard work too - there is no point in giving the impression that it is easy money as you could attract the wrong sort of people.

Draw the interview to a close when the applicant has no further questions and you have satisfied yourself that you have found out as much as you can about their suitability for the work. If you are still unsure then arrange to ring them later with your decision. This will give you time to think things over and possibly see other applicants who might help you make your mind up. If you're not sure, follow your instinct.

Once you have made a choice you can inform the successful applicant and arrange a mutually convenient time for them to attend for a full briefing.

Tony's Guide

Ask them to bring:

- ❑ Good evidence of their true identity (your you to copy and keep). A recent Utility Bill and a passport are perfect.

- ❑ Several passport sized pictures so that you can make an I.D badge

- ❑ Goods in transit and public liability insurance documents

- ❑ Driving related documents - driving licence, M.O.T certificate, certificate of insurance

- ❑ Bank details - name and address and phone number of branch, account number, sort code and name account is held in

- ❑ Next of kin name, address and phone number

- ❑ National insurance number.

- ❑ Local up-to-date street map of the immediate geographical area plus a U.K road atlas

- ❑ A mobile phone with plenty of credit and a 12v charger

Tony's Guide

Once you've got some customers, and some couriers to cover the work, you need make sure you to handle your callers the right way on the phone, or you'll have been wasting all that time and effort. This chapter covers how to keep them coming back time after time once they've signed up.

Accomplished use of the telephone is vital in your business as the many bookings are still placed by phone and it is the main point of contact between you and your customers. When you answer the phone you are the voice of your business.

The first impression a customer receives when they phone us up is the way in which the phone is answered.

❑　The Verbal Handshake

Answer the phone promptly, within 3 rings, and introduce yourself:

Begin with "Good Morning/Afternoon" - because it is polite and gives the caller a chance to tune in to your voice

Then introduce yourself and your business. A proven greeting is:

"Good Morning/Afternoon, CourierPlus, Tony speaking"

This avoids forcing your caller to ask, slightly wearily:

"Hi, who is that?"

People are more comfortable if they know who they are speaking to.

Develop a pleasant and clear speaking voice - your voice is your greatest asset on the phone, so using the right words, voice and tone will improve your communication skills.

Exuding calmness, confidence and competence - will reassure the customer that he has made the correct decision in phoning you.

Don't assume that because a customer puts you on hold that they cannot hear what you might say.

Don't "put your hand over the phone" to conceal what you are saying, as your caller can usually hear every word, and in any case it sounds really amateurish.

Be polite. Try to put a smile in your voice and answer warmly, speaking at a normal level and reasonable pace. If you are pleasant to your customers they will be pleasant with you, and are more likely to call again. Make friends with them.

Ask for and use the caller's name early in the conversation and frequently throughout. This making the person feel that the conversation you are having is personal to them.

Show interest - "How can I help?" shows enthusiasm and takes control of the conversation.

❑   Getting the point across

Communication consists of one person giving information and the other receiving it - one person speaking and the other listening.

Tony's Guide
to the courier industry

Listen - effective listening can save valuable time, effort and money and requires total concentration.

- ❑ be ready and willing to listen

- ❑ don't interrupt the customer

- ❑ use active listening phrases or words to prove you are still attentive

- ❑ record key words and information during the conversation

- ❑ never assume anything

Ask questions - clarify and expand the information given by the customer by asking further related "open ended" questions, e.g.

- ❑ "Do you have a contact name at the collection address?"

- ❑ "Have you a phone number for that site?"

- ❑ "Will we be able to gain access to the delivery site at that time of night?"

- ❑ "How heavy is the box?"

Stay assertive - even when you don't feel like it.

Offer help, and volunteer useful information - don't wait to be asked, for example:

- ❑ "For three pallets or more you'll need a Transit sized van". You need to know this kind of information about load sizes and weights.

- ❑ "I would advise you not to send tender documents with an overnight company, it would be much safer to send them with us".

- ❑ "I will ring our courier on his mobile and then call you back with an ETA"

- ❑ "I can hold if you need to answer that other call" - if you can hear another phone ringing in the background.

Don't be afraid to repeat yourself; check the detail, repeat the main points and summarise, so that you are both in no doubt as to what has been agreed.

Above all, know the name and phone number of your caller before you end the call. Then if all else fails you know you can get back to them and sort things out.

❏   Take action

Those queries or bookings which can be dealt with straight away, you should action immediately. Others can be more complex and require further information and more time; if you make a promise to take action or provide information by a certain time, you must keep that promise. Let the customer know even if the information still isn't available.

Put your name firmly on any promise you make:

"My name is Tony, and I'll call you back within 10 minutes"

If you just say "I'll call you back", your caller is left not knowing how long he has to wait to hear back from you.

❏   Control the conversation

If your caller begins to digress from the point of the call, choose a pause to interrupt politely, repeat the query or requirement and ask, in a closed question, if that is correct. In this way you can regain control and cut out the long story.

Get as much relevant information as you can. It will help you to determine exactly what the customer wants and how best to help them.

When taking bookings it is very important to get the information in the order you want it, so you can enter it into your pc, so ask for information in that order.

Do not keep customers on hold for more than a few seconds at a time as it can seem like an eternity, - you should ask them if they would like to hold in preference to being called back.

At the end of a call, always confirm what has been agreed.

❑ **Soothe your caller**

"Soothing" is any kind of attention you give to (or receive from) another person and it is a vital human need.

In your business the phone represents virtually our only way of "soothing" your customers - as you seldom meet them face-to-face.

The more pleasant your customers find the experience of placing a telephone booking with you - ie the more soothing they get - the more they will want to repeat the experience.

Here are some examples of general, easy soothing techniques which you can incorporate into your phone calls:

❑ Give a pleasant greeting

❑ Share a joke with them

❑ Compliment them

❑ Offer help - "How can I help you?"

❑ Use their name if the opportunity presents itself

❑ Thank them

In addition to these general examples there is another very important soothing technique which demands a more detailed explanation:

❑ **Speech style or tone:**

This involves making the caller feel even more comfortable by matching your speech style with theirs.

You should answer your call promptly within 3 rings and use a sensible greeting:

"Good Morning/Afternoon, CourierPlus, Tony speaking"

The caller will now introduce himself or herself and you should then instantly be able to make a decision about the tone or style in which you should then conduct the rest of the call. Your manner should approximate theirs.

In practice, dialogue with most customers will probably require a semi-formal speech style which should tread a comfortable path between the above two examples, being neither too stiff and starchy nor too chummy, something like:

"Hello Ann, yes I'll get a bike straight round, have you an address in Hartlepool?, Grantham Ltd, 100 Church Street, LN24, that's fine, right thanks Ann, bye!"

Tony's Guide

to the courier industry

Following on from the telephone technique we now put it all to good use, in taking bookings.

Telephone bookings are your lifeblood as a same day courier, so you have to handle them very carefully.

The positive benefits of perfectly taken bookings are many and the beneficiaries are your customers, your company, your employed staff and your couriers too. Everybody stands to gain from the booking being perfect in the first place, with no "introduced error".

High standards of service and efficiency will be guaranteed to your customers and following naturally from this - a smoother running, less stressful environment and daily experience for your operations staff and couriers, and a growing reputation for excellence.

Perfectly taken bookings are the start of:

- ❏ the maximum possible operational efficiency and therefore the highest attainable levels of service quality

- ❏ the impression of a quality operation

- ❏ perfect data and therefore detailed and accurate invoices - the information you record also forms the basis of the invoice you send

- ❏ loyalty from existing customers

- ❏ new sales generation - through existing customer recommendations

- ❏ greater company profitability, stability and sustained growth

- ❏ good staff morale - most people prefer working under less stress, and as part of a well-run team

- ❏ minimum numbers of invoice queries and credit notes

- ❏ minimum numbers of courier pay queries - and therefore maximum happy couriers

The booking process

We have established why we want to take a perfect booking, you have answered the call, given your greeting, listened to the caller's greeting, and decided on the tone for the rest of your speech.

Now you need to get the information and fill in whatever sort of booking form you are using.

❑ **Caller's name**

Always write down the name of the person making the call.

❑ **Service Type**

The type of service the customer needs eg motorcycle, small van, transit van etc. At the end of the booking repeat the service type to the caller to ensure it is correct.

Sometimes the caller will be unsure of what service type they need and you will have to use your common sense and experience to advise them. You will need to ask them:

Tony's Guide
to the courier industry

- How large the consignment is

- How heavy it is (the courier can refuse to take something too heavy for his vehicle)

- If the consignment is delicate

- How valuable the item is, carriage is safer in a van than on a bike.

- How urgent the job is, bikes are much faster through traffic.

- What the deadline is for the delivery.

Example:

A customer who rings and books a small van to transport a pallet of paper should be asked the weight of the consignment, as well as the dimensions, in case it overloads the van.

Example:

A customer rings to book an "overnight to London for 9am".

Firstly you must be sure what they mean by an "overnight". Do they want a dedicated vehicle to collect today and deliver the next morning or do they want a budget delivery of the type usually handled by a parcel company.

You should check that the consignment does not contain tender documents (or anything else with a crucial deadline), anything delicate/breakable, or anything valuable/irreplaceable.

If it does you should strongly advise the customer to send the item in one of your dedicated vehicles rather than a parcel service where there is a chance of it being damaged, late, or simply lost.

If you are interested in offering overnight parcel services to your customers, you should speak to MTvan.com, as there are opportunities to link up with established carriers on a wholesale basis, if you have freight to "input" into their systems. MTvan.com can put you in touch with the right people.

Everything described above should also be applied to enquiries for international jobs. There's good money to be made from these.

Tony's Guide

Tony's Guide
to the courier industry

This section describes in more detail how to enter a booking in MTvan.com. If you are using a paper-based system, or a pc-based computer system, many of the points made will still apply.

© Tim Gilbert 2005

Tony's Guide
to the courier industry

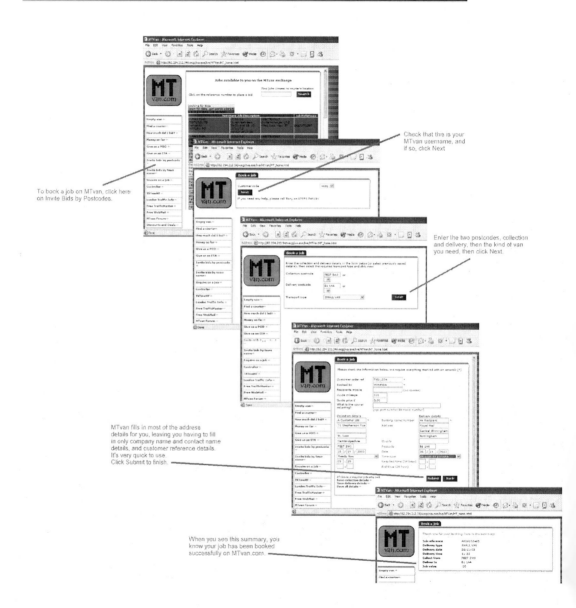

To book a job on MTvan, click here on Invite Bids by Postcodes.

Check that this is your MTvan username, and if so, click Next

Enter the two postcodes, collection and delivery, then the kind of van you need, then click Next.

MTvan fills in most of the address details for you, leaving you having to fill in only company name and contact name details, and customer reference details. It's very quick to use. Click Submit to finish.

When you see this summary, you know your job has been booked successfully on MTvan.com.

Tony's Guide

MTvan.com allows you to enter a booking with UK postcodes, and fills in the address of each postcode for you. This speeds up the process, leaving you only to add details such as company name and contact name in the address fields.

You can be comfortable about entering the full postcode, as on the MTvan page it will show only as the first element. Eg you enter "PE28 4NB" and it will display to those bidding as "PE28". So you don't need to worry about giving away the collection address to all and sundry.

You can also use "Town Names", though these take longer to book, as you have to fill in the address details yourself in full. It's also not as accurate for the purposes of calculating the "guide mileage" available on MTvan.com.

The Town Name method also needs a county code in this format: "OLDHAM, GM" where "OLDHAM" is the town name and ", GM" is Greater Manchester. Here is the list of counties:

GREAT BRITAIN

Avon	AV	Isles of Scilly	IS
Bedfordshire	BD	Kent	KT
Berkshire	BK	Lanarkshire	LK
Borders	BR	Lancashire	LA
Buckinghamshire	BM	Leicestershire	LT
Cambridgeshire	CB	Lincolnshire	LL
Central	CT	Lothian	LN
Channel Islands	CI	Merseyside	MS
Cheshire	CH	Mid Glamorgan	MG

Tony's Guide

Cleveland	CE	Norfolk	NK
Clwyd	CD	North Yorkshire	NY
Cornwall	CN	Northamptonshire	NN
County Durham	DU	Northern Ireland	NI
Cumbria	CU	Northumberland	ND
Derbyshire	DY	Nottinghamshire	NT
Devon	DN	Orkney	OK
Dorset	DT	Overseas	OS
Dumfries & Galloway	DG	Oxfordshire	ON
Dyfed	DD	Powys	PY
East Sussex	ES	Shetland	SD
Eire	EI	Shropshire	SP
Essex	EX	Somerset	ST
EUROPEAN UNION	EU	South Glamorgan	SG
Fife	FF	South Yorkshire	SY
Gloucestershire	GR	Staffordshire	SF
Grampian	GP	Strathclyde	SC
Greater London	GL	Suffolk	SK
Greater Manchester	GM	Surrey	SU
Gwent	GT	Tayside	TS
Gwynedd	GD	Tyne & Wear	TY
Hampshire	HP	Warwickshire	WK
Hereford & Worcestershire	HW	West Glamorgan	WG
Hertfordshire	HD	West Midlands	WM
Highland	HL	West Sussex	WS
Humberside	HS	West Yorkshire	WY
Isle of Man	IM	Western Isles	WI
Isle of Wight	IW	Wiltshire	WT

Tony's Guide

IRELAND

Co. Antrim	AN	Co. Limerick	LM
Co. Armagh	AM	Co. Londonderry	LD
Co. Carlow	CR	Co. Longford	LF
Co. Cavan	CV	Co. Louth	LU
Co. Clare	CL	Co. Mayo	MY
Co. Cork	CO	Co. Meath	MT
Co. Derry	DR	Co. Monaghan	MN
Co. Donegal	DL	Co. Offaly	OF
Co. Down	DO	Co. Roscommon	RC
Co. Dublin	DB	Co. Sligo	SL
Co. Fermanagh	FM	Co. Tipperary	TP
Co. Galway	GW	Co. Tyrone	TR
Co. Kerry	KR	Co. Waterford	WF
Co. Kildare	KD	Co. West Meath	WE
Co. Kilkenny	KK	Co. Wexford	WX
Co. Laois	LO	Co. Wicklow	WL
Co. Leitrim	LR		

If you want to use MTvan.com for courier work in the Republic of Ireland, or elsewhere in the EU, you have to use Town Names.

Questions about town names and county codes can be emailed to info@mtvan.com.

Or you can call our Members Hotline on 01948 667371.

Like most systems, MTvan.com allows you to save regular pick-up and delivery points. Once the address is programmed you need never type it in manually again. Programmed addresses make the   process of entering a job that much quicker and are of great benefit to new couriers too - if entered in a detailed form.

It is important for you that these address fields are filled in as accurately and in as much detail as possible, to save you operational and invoicing queries later. It also helps your chosen courier, as these details will appear on the POD sheet which the courier can print out once you have allocated the booking to the courier.

The minimum information which should be included in any address is:

- ❑ company name

- ❑ individuals name; if delivering to private address or as a contact at a company

- ❑ road or street name and number on same

- ❑ town name or postcode

Provided you get this lot, a courier should be able to find the address, if any of these are missing you should not confirm the booking but tactfully ask the customer for the missing components; you are not being awkward, just efficient. The only exception to this is if the caller genuinely does not have access to the information but promises that it will be provided with the consignment by the time the courier arrives to collect it. You should alert the controller to brief the courier not to leave without an adequate address and to make a full note of the address on the POD sheet so that you can enter the detail onto the job later.

Additional information which it is good practice to ask for, especially for private addresses, includes:

An example of a good address is shown below:

"ACME SAFE CO, 412 HIGH STREET, M1,0161 272 7777, (SEE CHRIS JONES) MANCHESTER, GM"

You will note this has six of the seven elements all squeezed onto the first line of the address leg - this is the ideal to aim for every time.

Residential addresses often have little detail, for instance:

"BOB SMITH, "ASH BANK FARM", TEL:01163 ****** ADRINGTON, CH"

This may be the complete address but could prove difficult to locate in a rural area with no street names or numbers. Therefore a phone number for the address is essential to help the courier to find the place. If the customer cannot provide one, point out the possibly difficulties which might be encountered, and see if any directions are available instead. Failing that, you could try the internet (eg www.streetmap.co.uk) or use directory enquiries service for a phone number as a last resort.

❑ **What is the courier collecting?**

The information entered here will be visible to your a courier as it will be printed out as a POD sheet from MTvan.com when you have allocated the booking to the courier you have chosen to do the job. It will also be visible when other courier members are bidding for your job.

The kind of messages which will be entered in this field will be things like:

❑ "if no one in at delivery leave round back under dustbin"

❑ "must deliver by 1700 - no fail!"

❑ "phone number at delivery is - *** *** *** "

❑ "package is very delicate, must handle with care! "

❑ "must only hand package to consignee - no one else!!"

❑ "have quoted 45 minutes for this pick-up"

❑ "two pallets, forklift available at collection and delivery"

If you want bids for your job, it helps people bid sensible prices and times if you give them extra details like this.

Tony's Guide
to the courier industry

❑ **Dates and Times:**

The key questions to ask initially are :

❑ "Is the consignment ready to go now?"

❑ "Is it to be delivered today and is there a deadline?"

If you have to change the date of either the collection or the delivery day then you must be alert enough to spot if either day falls on a weekend or a Bank Holiday - and double check with the caller that they are also cognisant of the fact as factors like surcharges may apply - which might affect their decision to book the job.

The overtime surcharges will affect all jobs booked for a collection between 1800 and 0800 hours. The surcharge is usually 50%.

Collections or deliveries made on these unusual days or at times outside the usual office ones can be problematical if you do not get enough information by asking the right questions at the outset.

Tony's Guide

to the courier industry

For unusual dates and times of pick-ups ask:

- ❑ "Are we expected at the collection point - will there be someone on-site?"

- ❑ "What are we to collect?"

- ❑ "Have you a contact name there who knows what we are collecting?"

- ❑ "Can I have the phone number of that site please?"

- ❑ "Can I have a phone number please so that we can call YOU or one of your colleagues if we run into difficulties with the collection?"

- ❑ "Are you aware that we charge overtime for a collection at that time?"

- ❑ For unusual dates and times of deliveries ask:

- ❑ "Will we be expected at the delivery point/s, - will there be someone on-site?"

- ❑ What would you like us to do if we arrive to find no one on site? -

- ❑ "try and leave the consignment with a neighbour? - we will of course leave a note at the proper address telling them where we have left it"

- ❑ "If there are no neighbours would you like us to -

- ❏ leave the consignment in a porch or other semi-secure location?

- ❏ post the consignment through the letterbox?

- ❏ keep the goods on board and re-deliver - when?

- ❏ ring you for further instructions?

Any information gained from these questions should be entered in the "What is the courier collecting/Comments".

Regarding pickup/delivery times: if you are asked to make a collection or delivery At, By or Between certain times you must be careful that to the best of your knowledge you will be able to fulfil the promise. If there is doubt that the promise can be fulfilled then you should advise the customer of this at the time of booking - or later if it becomes apparent after the booking has been confirmed. You should have no hesitation about doing this as it should be your policy to be open and honest at all times. Usually nothing is gained and everything lost by promising to deliver something which is in fact not possible.

Things to watch for when accepting the job include:

- ❏ requests for impossibly quick collections

- ❏ requests for impossibly quick job transit times

- ❑ requests to meet impossible deadlines for collections or deliveries

- ❑ requests for impossibly precise collection/delivery times

Same day courier work is not an exact science and so you should beware of guaranteeing anything too exact. For example:

If a customer asks you to provide a van to collect from somewhere at "exactly 1500 hours, not a minute early or a minute late!" you should advise him/her that "give or take a few minutes either side of course we can do that" - this allows for the traffic and other factors which are plainly out of your control.

Don't promise what you can't deliver. Better to promise slightly less than you know you can deliver, and deliver more than you've promised.

In the end the best solution when in doubt is to say that you will try but cannot guarantee to meet the promise. This way you will under-promise and over-deliver.

When advising a customer that you feel unable to meet their requests you should be polite, firm but not apologetic - after all if the request is impossible there is no reason to be.

So you might say something upbeat and cheerful like:

"I'm sorry we are very busy this afternoon so we cannot pick-up straight away, but we could be with you in about 20 minutes"

Tony's Guide

□ **Mileage**

Mileage shown on the booking is for guidance only. If you want to calculate exact mileages via specific routes, you can use AutoRoute, MapPoint, or go to The RAC or MultiMap on the internet

□ **Job Price**

This displays the price for the job calculated from the rate table relevant to the customer and is arrived at using the guide mileage calculated between the town names or postcodes. You can change the displayed mileage to a higher one, or you can manually alter the displayed price itself, but it's worth avoiding this as obviously it carries the risk of the customer receiving an invoice with price inconsistencies between bookings.

□ **Customer Reference**

On every booking you can ask the customer if they have a reference they would like to be entered in this field. Often they will have a numbers or letters which they would like entering here which will help them identify the job once they receive the invoice for it. If they have no reference enter their name in this field. There is space for 20 characters to be entered here.

It is important to try and get a reference for each job because it helps get invoices paid and get them paid more quickly.

❑   Entering a booking – final steps

Having taken all the details of the job from the caller and arrived at the option to "CONFIRM" the booking you should now run right back through all the details of the job - repeating them to the caller, for example:

"So David - you need a bike to collect a small envelope from your premises at Mill House, Mill Street, Cheadle, as soon as possible, and deliver it to the Warrington Guardian, 15 Bridge Street, Warrington. There is a 12 noon deadline on delivery and we must surrender the package only to Mr George Davies at the Guardian and will phone you with his POD and the time at which we obtained it as soon as possible afterwards - is that correct?"

You have now confirmed exactly what the caller requires and removed all doubt in both your minds. You can now go ahead and confirm the booking, by clicking on "Submit".

Here's how all this will look on MTvan.com. Just click on the "Invite Bids" link. It takes only a couple of minutes. You can enter the details of your job quickly and easily. Just enter the two postcodes...

Tony's Guide
to the courier industry

Book a job

Enter the collection and delivery details in the form below (or select previously saved details), then select the required transport type and click next

Collection postcode   [PE27 3WJ]   or

Delivery postcode   [B1 1AA]   or

Transport type   [SMALL VAN]   [Next]

Enter two postcodes and vehicle type, and click next

...then complete the details, and click on submit...

© Tim Gilbert 2005

Tony's Guide

to the courier industry

Book a job

Please check the information below. We require everything marked with an asterisk (*)

Customer order ref	(XYZ123)	*
Booked by	(CALLER'S NAME)	*

Put your phone number here if you want bids by phone

Recipients mobile		(no spaces)
Guide mileage	101	
Guide price £	0.00	
Comments	(PH BIDS 07976746191. 1 PALLET. 20 KGS)	

(eg: if you want bidders to phone you, you may enter your phone number here.)

Collection details

(PICKUP LTD)	*	Building name/number
Stephenson Road		Address
St. Ives		
Cambridgeshire		County
PE27 3WJ		Postcode
7 / 6 / 2004		Date
Ready Now ▾		Time type
14 : 49		Required time (24 hour)
:		End time (24 hour)

Delivery details

(DROP LTD)	*
1 ACACIA AVE	
Central Birmingham	
Birmingham	
B1 1AA	
7 / 6 / 2004	
By time entered below ▾	
18 : 00	
:	

Enter the details circled, click "submit", and that's it

If this is a regular job why not
Save collection details ➡
Save delivery details ➡
Save all details ➡

(**Submit** **Back**)

...and a summary of these details will appear on the MTvan exchange, coloured white:

Tony's Guide
to the courier industry

Jobs available to you on the MTvan exchange

Click on the reference number to place a bid.

Find jobs closest to courier's location

[ ] **Search**

Looking for Bids
Open for Bids, got some already
Bidding closed, job covered

Click on these links to bid

Summary Job Description			Job Reference
Collect from WARWICK, WK Deliver to PRESCOT, MS	09/06/04 Ready now 09/06/04 ASAP	7.5 TONNE TRUCK Guide mileage: 121 Miles from you:	AF09103413
Collect from SOUTHAM, WK Deliver to YEADON, WY	11/06/04 Collect after 13:00 11/06/04 ASAP	7.5 TONNE TRUCK Guide mileage: 143 Miles from you: 11	AF11000746
Collect from NE625HE Deliver to PAISLEY	09/06/04 Collect at 09:00 09/06/04 ASAP	By Small Van Guide mileage: 156 Miles from you: 13	AF09004412
Collect from COVENTRY CV6 Deliver to COVENTRY CV2	09/06/04 Ready now 09/06/04 ASAP	Guide mileage: 4 Miles from you: 14	AF09008902
Collect from COVENTRY CV2 Deliver to	09/06/04 Ready now 09/06/04	Guide mileage: 33 Miles from you: 16	AF09008903

(The full details of your job are automatically hidden for you, so you know you're not giving away the details of your customers to all and sundry).

As soon as you see this summary, you know that details of your booking are being **texted** and emailed to any Members based or empty in the area.

If you are happy to receive bids by phone, you can put your own phone number in the "Comments" box.

Members will bid for the job by clicking on the link as shown above, offering you a price and a time. The job will then turn light blue.

It's up to you how long you choose to leave the job open for bids, and who you choose to give the job to. Details of all bids received are emailed to you, and texted to your mobile, complete with phone numbers of bidders, so you can get in touch with them direct and give them the job.

You then go back into MTvan.com, and allocate the job to the successful bidder, using the "Controller" link.

This will turn the job dark blue, so others know that bidding is closed. It will also enable the successful bidder to log and download a POD sheet (click on the job number in "Give us a POD"), if this makes sense, and later to log in and enter a POD for you.

Do be sure to discuss payment terms with your successful bidder, when agreeing the details of the job on the phone. Obviously, you can't afford to get a reputation for being a bad payer on MTvan.com, as people will be reluctant to bid on your work. You can also invite bids for courier work to and from the continent, as many of our British couriers are available at very short notice for collections especially in France, Spain, Benelux and Germany. Use town names, not postcodes, to book these.

Tony's Guide
to the courier industry

❑ General Enquiries

Enquiries for details of your services are best referred to your salesman. If you have no person with such a specific role then listen carefully and make notes of what information the caller requires. If it is possible to provide the information, agree to do so. You can fax it while the caller is still on the phone. Alternatively send a hard copy in the post, or arrange for it to be dropped off by courier, or best of all, visit them yourself to deliver it.

Be sure that the caller is interested in same day courier services as opposed to an overnight or next day service as this will save you both a lot of wasted time.

Ask if they require prices for any specific regular journeys so that you can include them in your information.

Always make it clear that the prices you quote whether verbally or in writing are understood to be exclusive of VAT.

❑ Enquiries from Existing Customers

More immediate enquiries will come from existing customers who may need to know the cost of one or more jobs that you have already completed for them, but for which they have not yet been invoiced. You can enquire on MTvan.com, "enquire on a job", print it out, and offer to fax them a report, or paste it into an email.

© Tim Gilbert 2005

Or they may want to know the cost of one or more jobs they are thinking of booking in the future and for which they need to know the cost in advance. These can be answered by doing a dummy booking using their account code - this will give you a price for the job.

If you are very busy then it can be as well to point out to the caller that while at this moment you have a vehicle available to collect in so many minutes that may not be the case if they call back later due to the current high level of demand for your services. This reminds the customer of the way the business is run and may encourage them to either book straight away or pre-book a van - either way the customer will be able to make an informed decision based on what you have told them and should not be disappointed.

When entering a dummy booking for quotation purposes you need not be insistent on exhaustive address details but you still must be careful with regard to the accuracy of the key points:

- ❏ vehicle/service type
- ❏ pickup town name
- ❏ collection time
- ❏ delivery time
- ❏ transit time

As all these points will directly affect the feasibility of the job itself and in some cases the cost of the job too. How busy you are may also play a part. If demand is currently high always consult with the controller before quoting on a job or if you are sufficiently experienced make a decision yourself.

❏ **New Account Enquiries**

Enquiries from non-account holders can be handled in a similar way. You can use an existing customer's code in order to quote on a job.

If a non-account holding caller decides they would like to go ahead with the booking having approved of your quote then we suggest the following:

> ❏ Insist politely on receiving the details of their first job on a faxed piece of their letterhead. This must include all the usual information which you need when taking a booking.
>
> ❏ Make sure they realise that you need to receive the above before you will despatch the vehicle.

Ensure also that during this first conversation you say something like the following:

"Although we are of course happy to do this first job for you without formality we will be posting you an Account Application/Conditions of Carriage form which you need to complete, sign and return to our office so that proper credit facilities can be set up"

When the fax arrives get a courier to copy down the details from the fax, if necessary. This ensures that the job gets under way as soon as possible.

Set up an account for the new customer from the details provided on the fax.

Enter the job on the newly established account code from the details on the fax.

Send the Application form off to them first class or get the courier to drop it off when he collects, along with a brief covering letter which explains its purpose.

Send an introductory information pack thanking the customer for booking the first job and welcoming them aboard - the Application form can be enclosed with this if it does not go with the courier.

Keep their faxed letterhead for at least 3 months as it is good evidence that they ordered the services which it describes.

Alert whoever is doing your credit controlling if the customer looks like becoming a large account who intend to spend a lot quickly and whose creditworthiness therefore needs checking out immediately.

❑ **Complicated quotes:**

These may require more thought and include:

- large multidrops

- the provision of a number of dedicated "contract vehicles" for a given time period - temporary or permanent

- direct deliveries abroad

- air courier jobs

- regular "standing order" type jobs

We recommend that unless you are very sure of yourself that you do not quote over the phone straight away. Check out all the costs involved in the job first and ring the caller back once you have arrived at a price which includes a sensible margin. For very involved quotes you should ask for written or faxed details from the caller so that you can be sure you know all that is involved before committing yourself to a price. If there is still room for confusion or misinterpretation on receipt of the information ring to clarify and if necessary ask for a fresh amended copy to be sent to you before you quote.

Jobs requiring a van and driver for a large amount of time but involving little actual mileage should be charged at an hourly rate beginning at £20 per hour for a small van, depending on what is the going rate in your area.

❑ Pricing

When quoting a price for a job the usual common-sense approach as with most areas of selling is to start with a price slightly higher than the one you would be happy to end up at; this way you can always 'discount' down to this figure if the caller thinks the initial quote too high.

Use a tone of voice, and a form of words that encourage the customer to spend the money. Don't be ashamed to charge for your services. Use a bright and encouraging tone of voice to announce the price, to make them feel good about accepting it:

"From you to Birmingham by small van? That's a mere £120 plus the VAT, and we can do that for you immediately".

It's very easy to make the mistake of saying it in a way that will make your caller feel foolish if they accept your price:

"Blimey, I'm afraid that's £120"

When you get to the stage of employing people in your control room, you should listen out for this, and train it out of new recruits, as it can seriously reduce the amount of work you get.

❑ Summary:

In all cases of enquiries and quotations you should be polite and helpful.

Do not be tempted to quote below the minimum price you are comfortable with.

Your customers want to be made to feel that they are important, so they demand respect and good manners. They want to feel that you are interested in them, so they expect you to show that you really are interested.

They want to know what is in it for them, and how they will benefit from choosing your service. So they expect us to listen to them, and to discuss things from their point of view. In short, they expect good Customer Care.

Customer Care provides both a challenge and an opportunity.

A challenge...because customers expect good care - if you don't look after your customers, someone else will.

An opportunity...for you to offer more than your competitors - you will be setting the pace in the market place, and they will have to work harder to catch up.

❑ What is Customer Care?

It is both caring for customers and caring about them.

This is about a serious, unseen threat to your business. It is about the customers you nearly had, the ones you should have had, but allowed, or even encouraged, to drift away to your competitors, but never knew about; the ones you did have, but lost without realising they had gone, the so called lapsed customers who will never return.

© Tim Gilbert 2005

Tony's Guide

to the courier industry

Who are these silent people you never knew about? The ones who had it in their power to strengthen your business and make it grow, but chose not to? Where did they go to, and why? The ones who had the power of life or death over you business, but quietly walked away, never to return, who stay silently in the world of might-have-been and who could, had they so wished, have transformed your business?

The disturbing fact is that they didn't just go. You sent them away. You made them feel that they were not welcome, they were not valued. Not in so many words of course, but this was their perception. You assumed they would be quite happy with service and attention, which they felt was merely average. Nobody seemed particularly interested in them, wanted to help them or find out what they wanted. Some of them were made to feel they were a bit of a nuisance. So they made their protest in the only way they could.

By walking away.

Getting customers and keeping them are the only parts of your courier business that create income. All other activities create costs. Intense competition often means that customers have a choice between many suppliers of identical or very similar courier services. You and your closest competitors are probably using very similar vans, couriers, clothing, prices, invoicing systems, and so on. This makes it hard for you to create noticeable difference between you and your competitors. Customer Care can be your noticeable difference. And in many cases, it's free.

For example, the difference between you and your competitor could be as simple as your customer being able to say: "We have confidence in everything you tell us".

Tony's Guide
to the courier industry

□ How do Customers make that choice?

Increasingly, customers choose on the basis of emotional factors (like after-sales service, speed of collection, and attitude of staff) that surround the service itself, rather than on the service itself. Customer satisfaction or dissatisfaction comes more and more from the way the person is treated, ie from the customer care.

So, better customer care gives your business the opportunity to be "special". It provides the means whereby you can stand head and shoulders above your competitors in the marketplace. You can win more customers and keep them loyal to you.

Whenever a customer comes into contact with a courier company - face to face, by phone, in writing, or on the internet, their image of the courier company is being established. Staff are perceived as representing not just themselves but the entire organisation.

Customers' perceptions are emotional, idiosyncratic and sometimes irrational. Often they are based on a narrow observation - "If that's a swallow, it must be summer" or "You can always tell a good courier by how clean his van is" - but customers' perceptions determine your business success or failure.

If you treat your customers badly, it will make them unhappy. The customers will retaliate and make you unhappy. And it won't do your profits a lot of good either.

So you need to ask yourself how to get it right. What sort of care and attention should you give to the customer?

If you make your customers happy, they will respond in kind. That will make your profits happy. And on it will go because, if you are successful, you and your staff and couriers, are much more likely to be happy and get satisfaction from your contribution.

Customers' expectations of service are rising. Customers are now are more conscious of the way they are being treated and expect a better level of service.

Who are the easiest people to sell to?

For most courier companies it is existing customers - they know you and your company. They trust it. They will buy again - provided that they continue to receive distinctive service. You have to work ensure that this is what they think about you.

Which is the next easiest group of people to sell to?

It's the people those customers recommend to – their friends, relatives or colleagues.

Your existing customers are crucial to your future success – so it follows that they should get exceptional care.

❑ Behaviour and Attitude

People behave like a mirror. They respond in kind; it's as if they are saying, "And the same to you". Friendly behaviour brings friendly behaviour; "Thank you for calling".

Curt unpleasantness brings more of the same reaction, leaving them wanting to say "…And drop dead yourself" at the end of the call.

Tony's Guide

to the courier industry

Behaviour is a choice - you can choose your behaviour. You don't have to be a prisoner of it. Something may have happened to make you feel angry, sad or unhappy. And you're about to talk to a customer. Before you do that, try saying to yourself, "I'm going to smile and pretend I'm happy". After a minute or two, you find that the customer is a very pleasant person to talk to. They thank you warmly for the help you have given them - and you start to feel happier.

Occasionally a customer is aggressive with you and starts to blame you for someone else's mistake. You could follow your natural inclinations and be aggressive in return. Or you can choose to be patient and remain pleasant. You will probably find that their aggression will dissipate like steam from a kettle. And they will apologise for venting their anger on you.

Behaviour is a choice. You can select behaviour that will help you deal with the customer, or select behaviour that will hinder you.

❑ **What behaviour should you choose?**

When dealing with customers, your behaviour should be:

❑ **Professional**:

Your personal feelings should be put aside. You should leave your worries and strife in a parcel outside the door when you go in to work. If you want to, you can collect them again on your way home.

© Tim Gilbert 2005

□ Understanding:

You are in a "people" business. They want help, and solutions to their problems. That's what they're buying from you. They will turn to you for that help and give you their business if you can show them that you fully understand their situation.

□ Be patient:

Yes, it may be a stupid question that the customer has just asked. And you may have already answered it 50 times this week. But it may well be the first time this customer has asked it. So be patient.

□ What attitude should you adopt?

Take responsibility for helping the customer. Own the problem, until it is solved, then own the satisfaction for having helped out.

The right attitude is to take responsibility for sorting out what the customer wants. The wrong attitude is to pass the buck or blame onto someone else in your business.

Your customers want help, not to be passed from pillar to post. And it's important that they see your company as a team who all care and want to help. They don't want to be faced with bickering, blaming or buck-passing.

Tony's Guide

- ❑ Be enthusiastic, it's contagious.

- ❑ Be confident, it increases a potential customer's trust in you.

- ❑ Be welcoming, it satisfies the customer's basic human desire to feel liked and approved of.

- ❑ Be helpful, customers want that more than anything else.

- ❑ Be polite, and always be well mannered.

- ❑ Show you care, make all customers feel they are important individuals.

❑ Assertiveness:

Assertive behaviour means:

❑ standing up for your rights without violating their rights.

❑ stating your views whilst showing that you understand their views.

❑ not blaming, but instead seeking the right solution.

❑ enhancing yourself without diminishing them.

❑ you win but they don't lose.

❑ talking calmly.

❑ making brief statements.

❑ asking open questions to find out what they want. Typically these will begin with "What", "Why", "Who" "When and "Where"

❑ separating fact and opinion, eg "I agree that we must do it, but your approach isn't the only way"

❑ avoiding phrases like "You should", "You ought". "You must", "You've got to".

❑ seeking acceptable solutions, eg "Let's have a look at how we can resolve this".
❑ keeping your voice: steady, sincere, calm.

- ❑ keeping your speech fluent whilst emphasising key words.

- ❑ keeping your facial expression open and steady.

- ❑ keeping eye contact steady.

- ❑ keeping other body language in agreement: head up, hands open.

❑ **Assertive behaviour when faced with conflict:**

Conflict tends to bring out basic natural instincts to stand and fight (aggression) or run and hide (submission). Aggression can make us feel good and have a sense of power. But the long-term effects can be detrimental. Assertive behaviour can be better than both.

❑ **Treat others as equals:**

Recognise their abilities and limitations rather than regarding them as superiors (submissive) or inferiors (aggressive).

❑ **Greater self-responsibility:**
Instead of blaming others (aggressive) or constantly saying "sorry" (submissive) you take responsibility for yourself and for achieving what you want to achieve.

❑ **Greater self-control:**
Your mind is concentrated on achieving the behaviour you want. You aren't submitting to control by others. And you haven't given in to an emotional aggressive outburst.

❑ It can produce a win-win situation:

Both people's opinions are given a fair hearing - so both can feel they have won. Aggressive or submissive behaviour is likely to result in win-lose, which inevitably becomes lose-lose.

❑ The telephone.

A two-minute phone call, if it is badly handled, can destroy the effect of thousands of pounds of advertising, hours of sales effort, or years of good reputation. The phone is the most important part of your customer care strategy since virtually all dealings with your customers are made through it - so it is important that it is used well, this means applying the ideas we've already discussed and those described in the Telephone Technique section.

Tony's Guide
to the courier industry

Here are of some of the key points:

- ❑ Keep good records of your conversations

- ❑ Smile as you speak

- ❑ Give all your attention to the customer

- ❑ Get their name, note it down, and use it

- ❑ Ask plenty of questions (especially open ones)

- ❑ Listen hard and show them you are listening

- ❑ Keep your voice interesting by varying the speed and emphasis

- ❑ Pause, to show you are thinking about what they have said

- ❑ Keep it fresh - remember that they are individuals, not part of a crowd

- ❑ Use clear, vivid expressions

- ❑ Cut out superfluous phrases (eg "you know")

- ❑ At the end of the conversation, summarise what you have agreed.

However tempting it is to avoid the discomfort of handling complaints, it is worth going through the pain. Most dissatisfied customers do not go back and complain, but they do tell lots of other people how bad you are. Most will never return.

It generally costs many times as much to attract a new customer as it does to keep an existing one.

> ❏ **The key messages are:**

Encourage customers to complain, as you can't sell to them if you're not talking to them.

Handle their complaints beautifully, and turn people who complain into ambassadors. Imagine someone hearing this said about your business:

"Like anyone, they're not perfect all the time, but when they mess up, they certainly do everything imaginable to fix the problem".

> ❏ **How to turn angry, awkward or complaining customers into ambassadors:**

People complain when they haven't got what they expected. Their dissatisfaction has probably been bottled up and shaken. Take the top off and it comes whooshing out.

Some people feel (wrongly) that the way to handle it is to push the top back on and shake it some more. In other words, stop them talking and get annoyed yourself.

If only they had the empathy to put themselves in the other person's shoes, they would soon see how crass that approach is.

Tony's Guide

Don't:

- ❑ say "It's not my fault".

- ❑ say "You're the fifth today to complain about that".

- ❑ interrupt. It will only add to their anger.

- ❑ jump to conclusions.

- ❑ accept responsibility until you're sure it's your fault.

- ❑ be patronising.

- ❑ argue.

- ❑ lose your temper.

- ❑ blame others.

Tony's Guide

to the courier industry

Do:

- ❏ show empathy and use appropriate body language (eg show concern on your face, nod).

- ❏ use their name.

- ❏ listen and use body language to show that you are listening (eg eye contact).

- ❏ take notes.

- ❏ let them make their case - they will lose their head of steam.

- ❏ ask questions to clarify the details.

- ❏ go back over it; confirm with them that you've got it right.

- ❏ sympathise (regardless of where the blame lies).

- ❏ gather together your version of the facts before replying.

- ❏ phone back if necessary - on time!

- ❏ apologise profusely if you are at fault.

- ❏ list alternatives for them to choose from, if you are at fault.

- ❏ do more than the bare minimum (eg make some concession on future business).

- ❏ get their full agreement that this will resolve the issue.

- ❏ make sure this it is done properly and that they are kept.

fully informed.

❑ contact them very soon afterwards to make sure that they are happy.

❑ see it as an opportunity to cement the relationship and encourage more business.

If you handle their complaint well, you will have made the customer feel important. They will want to praise your company to their friends. And they will be prepared to do business with you again. It's so much easier, quicker, and cheaper than having to go and get a new customer to replace the disappointed one.

Tony's Guide

to the courier industry

"Profit in business comes from repeat customers, customers that boast about your project or service, and that bring friends with them".
- W EDWARDS DEMING

Tony's Guide

It's always useful to have some part time freelance couriers who you can call upon to cover any jobs during periods of excess demand. This is where MTvan.com can really help you. With hundreds of members throughout the UK, the majority of them owner drivers, MTvan.com allows you to keep your own fleet to the minimum size for the amount of work you have, while still being able comfortably to cover all your work.

There's no need to turn work down, which can be very damaging. Instead, tell the customer that you're happy to take the job on, and you just have to make a few enquiries as to how long it will be to collect. You can then put the job on MTvan.com, and wait for bids to arrive from MTvan members. MTvan.com will text details of your job to nearby Members, so you should get offers very quickly.

If your customer is happy with "first thing tomorrow morning", this work is especially well suited for MTvan.com. The best prices bid on MTvan.com are often for "first thing tomorrow" bookings. This allows you to keep your own fleet available for the usual work booked in the morning, while still paying a sensible price for the pre-bookings from the day before.

Tony's Guide

to the courier industry

Controlling

It's the job of the "controller" (sometimes called the "Despatcher") to match the customers' needs with the couriers' availability. It takes a lot of skill and experience to do the job well.

Controlling Techniques

Controlling is a highly individual skill - two equally competent controllers might have wildly contrasting styles and yet still both produce excellent results. Therefore it is not possible to specify a single right or wrong way of going about the job. There are however some basic objectives which can be stated:

- ❑ quick pick-up times

- ❑ quick transit and delivery times

- ❑ POD phone/fax-backs

- ❑ information phonebacks

All of these objectives if met will result in a very high standard of service to each customer - a sure way of retaining a loyal customer base as well as benefiting from its priceless by-product - new customers who come by recommendation.

These objectives, in detail, are:

❑   Quick pick-up times

This is the foremost thing the customer will notice about the service they receive. The quicker the consignment is collected the quicker it should arrive, they assume. Once it's left their office, they feel as though you're well on your way to solving their problem.

❑   Quick journey times

This is the second thing the customer notices and judges the service quality by. Obviously the sooner the job is delivered the better the service quality is. From the customer's point of view, it's all about reputation, based on customer perception.

From your point of view, the sooner the job is completed the sooner that courier is again available to do more work; the sooner the job is completed the sooner the POD phone/fax/email-back can be made; the quicker each job is, the more jobs get done. The more jobs which get done, the more each courier turns over. The more each courier turns over the more money you and your couriers will make and the happier you all will be. It's called productivity.

❑   POD confirmation by phone/fax/email

When the job has been delivered it's worth ringing/faxing/emailing a customer to give the POD (proof of delivery) complete with time of delivery. This lets the customer know that their consignment has arrived safely and in good time and is particularly important for long-distance jobs with a deadline. If you can't do it on every job, you should aim to make a call or an email on every job over 20 miles, whether the customer asks for it or not, as it proves to them the quality of service they are buying from you.

❑   Keeping your customer informed

Tony's Guide

Generally, you should try to keep the customer informed of any developments before, during or after their job. Examples of this could be:

- ❏ you are sorry to disturb them, but your courier is running 10 minutes late on their collection but will be with them by <time as appropriate>.

- ❏ your courier is being kept waiting at the remote collection point, and you will let them know when he has collected successfully

- ❏ your courier has arrived at the collection point but no one on-site knew what he was supposed to be collecting, but he's resolved it now and is on his way, with an ETA of…

- ❏ there has been a multiple pile-up on the M1 and your courier although not directly involved is currently sitting in stationary traffic

- ❏ your courier has arrived at the delivery site but there appears to be no one there - is it ok for us to post the consignment?

These examples whilst not perhaps seeming good news are nearly always welcomed by the customer as they then feel (quite rightly) that they are dealing with a professional company.

They appreciate that you take the extra effort to keep them informed of events which may have far-reaching effects upon themselves and/or their business. You are giving them every chance of reacting to the new circumstances as they occur. So generally this procedure of keeping your customers informed cannot be overdone. Let them know you're solving their problem.

To help them believe you, mention that you are checking on the traffic delays reported by your courier on one of these websites:

www.bbc.co.uk/travelnews/
www.theaa.com/travelwatch/travel_news.jsp
www.highways.gov.uk/trafficinfo/

It is better to inform a customer of a delay in the collection of their consignment - even if this results in them cancelling the job in favour of a competitor, as the customer will respect and trust you all the more for it and will book more work in the future for this very reason.

Generally "honesty is the best policy". The only exceptions to this are where perhaps the volunteering of certain information might result in significant financial decrement and/or precipitate legal action against your business or one of its employees. If this is the case, just clam up, make notes immediately about every detail of the incident, and consult your lawyer.

Tony's Guide

to the courier industry

The job/s having arrived on your control desk now need to be given out to a courier.

Remember a first class service to the customer is your overriding concern and arranging a quick pick-up time on the job/s is the first priority with which you should concern yourself.

It is common sense that the closest available courier to the collection point is the one who is most likely to achieve the fastest pick-up time and this is the basic policy which should govern your decisions about which of several couriers you allocate to a particular job.

There are however other factors which need to be considered at the same time as who is closest:

- ❏ the closest courier may not be familiar with the pick-up point while another further away is and may actually pick-up quicker than his closer colleague

- ❏ the closest courier may, in your experience, be slower overall in doing jobs than a faster colleague who is a little further from the pick-up point. The point here is that the closer, slower courier may collect a little quicker but actually take longer overall to complete the job than a quicker courier who might collect ten minutes later but complete the job thirty minutes earlier. This factor should be remembered for long distance jobs in particular, especially if they have a deadline.

- ❑ the closest courier to the pick-up may not be able to do the job for a variety of reasons: he/she may have one or more jobs on board already which would not "fit in" with the extra one; he/she may have a vehicle capable of transporting the job but is still unfit to do it; he/she may have booked time off with you which will preclude him/her from being able to complete it - but in all these case you can ask the courier to collect the package and relay it on to someone who is able to do the job. In this way you can still effect a quick pick-up time and probably speed the job on its way to its final destination into the bargain. This is an advanced controlling technique.

- ❑ couriers who are very experienced and utterly competent in the job as a whole are often the correct choice for the first job for a new customer or a particularly time-sensitive, complex, or otherwise "difficult" job and should be chosen in preference to a less experienced courier. Even if they are significantly further away from the pick-up they usually make up for this in completing the job more efficiently overall.

- ❑ during quiet periods when there is a lull in demand it is good practice to operate a queuing system for the couriers so that the next job is given to the courier who has been "standing by" for the longest period of time. If this courier is standing by close to the pick-up point anyway then so much the better. If, however, he is significantly further away than another courier who is also standing by or simply passing the collection point then you should come to a decision based on the urgency of the job. If the job is extremely urgent then the closest person should get it, if it is not then the "next-out" courier should be offered it.

❏ **Courier Earnings**

Another factor which on occasion might be considered, but only if the service quality to the customer is not in any way compromised, is the matter of courier earnings. Part of your job as a controller is to maintain the loyalty and of your regular couriers, as this will enhance still further the service quality provided while at the same time making both yours and their job more pleasant and rewarding.

If all else is equal and you have a choice of several couriers all similarly close to the pick-up and all similarly competent and quick, you might like to consider which of them has earned the least lately. It's usually the case that one of them has had a poor week, through bad luck and/or no lack of their own efforts, and could most do with the extra money which the job you have represents.

The idea here of course is that helpful, competent couriers, who feel they are respected and considered properly, are a huge asset to your business, and a priceless blessing to you as a controller.

Keeping your regular couriers happy at the same time as maintaining the highest standards of service quality is at the heart of good controlling.

❏ Creative Controlling

What we have looked at so far are the basics of controlling and the factors which should govern your decision as to which single courier to give which single job. As soon as you have more bookings than you have available couriers, you'll need to be creative.

If your company has only three couriers or if it has thirty the principle is the same. As soon as demand outstrips supply, as soon as all three or all thirty couriers are occupied, and the forth or thirty-first job comes in, you need to shift your controlling up a gear.

You'll need to make the most of your regular couriers, and call in some extras as short notice. This is where MTvan.com can really help you. Just enter the job, and Invite Bids from the other courier Members. MTvan.com will text details of your job to nearby couriers, so you should get the quick response you need.

Just because you have one, two, three or fifteen jobs to cover, and no regular couriers left, it does not necessarily spell disaster. Rather, it proves there is a healthy demand for your services and so in many ways the situation of demand just slightly exceeding supply is an ideal to aim for. You just need to plan for it.

For example, if you know you will be short of couriers tomorrow, you can start by putting all your "pre-bookings" for tomorrow onto MTvan.com, to leave your own fleet as free as possible.

Similarly, if you have pre-bookings for later in the day, and you're already short of couriers, start inviting bids from other MTvan.com Members right away, to give yourself more options.

Tony's Guide
to the courier industry

The key essentials here are forward thinking and planning.

Forward thinking and planning are the most important tools to employ during busy periods of controlling.

Keep a list of what your regular couriers are doing, and when and where you expect them to become available. Keep updating it, as new information comes in from them. This allows you to check quickly your availability as new bookings come in, so you know what you can promise your customers.

Then put any booking you can't immediately cover onto MTvan.com, to invite bids from other courier members.

If there is no prospect of a reasonably quick pick-up time for the job you or a colleague should ring the customer and advise them of the estimated best possible pick-up time. This allows them to decide whether they still wish you to go ahead with the collection. It's better to lose the job and preserve your reputation, than to keep the job.

But be sure you have covered every angle before you do ring and quote a delay on the pick-up as it could result in a cancelled booking.

❑ Relaying & Doubling Up

We have touched on relaying a little above and it is simply the process of getting one courier to collect a consignment in order to relay it onto another who for whatever reason is better placed or suited to continue with the delivery.

© Tim Gilbert 2005

Tony's Guide

Doubling up is another way of covering outstanding work - but with couriers who already have one or more jobs on board. The principle is simple: if for example you have a courier who has just collected a package in W1 going WC2 and you have another identical outstanding job it is common sense to give that courier the second job too.

He/she will be happy as he/she will be earning twice the money, you will be happy as you have covered a previously outstanding job and both customers will be happy too as both deliveries will be completed in scarcely more time than one on its own.

It becomes even more important that you double up if the job is a long-distance one and when you are busy, as if you do not you will "lose" two couriers for a large amount of time instead of one. This could well leave you short of couriers to cover other work which comes in subsequently. Good controlling is all about forward planning and ensuring that you maximise the earnings potential of each courier and therefore of your business.

Very competent, quick, experienced couriers can do three, four, five, six and even more jobs all at the same time - and all without delaying each individual job unduly.

A word of warning however about doubling up. You must choose the correct courier for this as not all are capable of doing it quickly and efficiently.

Certain jobs with extremely tight deadlines should not be doubled up if at all possible for obvious reasons. Better to arrange something else, such as an extension of the delivery deadline on one of the deliveries, or Invite Bids on the less urgent one.

❏ Ask couriers to stand by near your customers

This technique is useful during lulls in demand on a generally busy day as a courier standing by will usually respond much more quickly to a collection than someone sitting in a courier room. You can ask couriers to stand-by in strategic locations near concentrations of customers, or close to important or busy customers who you know will be ringing you soon to book a courier.

Standing by close to customers is as important on quiet days for the same reasons as above , as it is just as important to keep service quality high on quiet days as on busy ones.

Couriers can sometimes stand-by at home where they may be able to keep occupied with other things and will probably feel happier.

Some of your couriers may find work from other courier companies at the times when you have no work to offer them. You should encourage this, as it increases their earnings, and reduces the risk of the Inland Revenue challenging your claim that the courier is not an employee.

Tony's Guide

to the courier industry

Tony's Guide

Motivating your regular couriers

A courier who has been working non-stop since first thing might well be flagging by half way through the afternoon, and be reluctant to carry on without a break.

Of course people must have a chance to stop for a break now and again as is only right - for many reasons, and foremost amongst them is the safety aspect. Driving safely for long periods of time requires immense concentration and is therefore very tiring. So of course you must allow couriers to grab a coffee and a sandwich.

Try and arrange a mutually agreeable compromise by asking the courier if it would be possible for him/her to at least collect the outstanding job/s first and then grab a bite to eat before setting of to deliver them.

Tony's Guide

to the courier industry

The moment you realise you haven't got a courier immediately available, you should look on MTvan.com. You can find out if couriers from other courier members are near your outstanding booking or will be soon - and could therefore be invited to bid for the job. The simplest thing is to invite bids from other courier members. They will then tell you how close they are to your collection, and what price they can offer.

Ideally, you should aim to have enough couriers immediately available to keep them busy pretty much all the time, and use MTvan.com for your excess. This way, your couriers are always busy, and your customers are always kept happy. If you're worried about giving your work away to people you don't know, which is understandable, check out their "approvals" in the Find a Courier Directory on MTvan.com.

Many Members have "Trusted Status", showing that other Members are happy to trust them with their work. Members with the most "Trusted Status" with other Members are shown at the top.

Members can also update their own details with their insurance cover and fleet size, for you to inspect.

For maximum reassurance, use the "Track this Member" feature. This allows you, with the Member's permission, to track their actual position, so you can be as confident about giving a job to an MTvan Member as you can about giving one to your own fleet.

© Tim Gilbert 2005

❏   Anticipation and planning

You should plan to maintain adequate levels of high quality full time and part time couriers monitor holiday/time off arrangements so that you do not have not have too many couriers off at the same time.

Pay particular attention to time off booked for Fridays, the last week of any given month, the Friday before a Bank Holiday weekend, and the whole of December before Christmas. Anything you cannot cover can be posted on MTvan.com to invite bids on it from other members.

❏   Courier numbers

Achieving and maintaining an adequate number of high quality couriers to cover all possible levels of demand each day, year in year out is the challenge to be met as this is how your courier business with grow.

This challenge cannot be answered by over-manning with regular couriers, as this brings its own problems.

The first thing a courier will notice is a reduction of his earnings. This will lower his morale and therefore his loyalty to your business. This will have the knock-on effect of lowering the service quality the customers receive and which may cause some of them to decide to take their business elsewhere too.

Office staff morale will suffer too due to the extra stress involved with a high turnover of couriers.

The alternative to over-staffing with full-time couriers is to maintain sufficient numbers of them to cover an average day but have in reserve some reliable part-time people or agents upon whom you can call when demand does go through the roof. You can find these reserve couriers on MTvan.com. This gets avoids having to make a choice between happy couriers and happy customers. You can have both if you have enough trusted people in your reserve.

Tony's Guide

Tony's Guide

❑ Waiting time

The idea behind this charge is to discourage customers from booking a courier long before they are ready for him - and that if they do there is a charge for the privilege which in some small measure will compensate both company and courier for his period of otherwise non-earning inactivity.

The charge is usually waived if a courier is kept waiting for less than 15 minutes. If the wait is longer than 15 minutes, usually the charge is then made for that 15 minutes and for every subsequent minute thereafter.

Not charging for anything less than 15 minutes allows your customers a little "free" time to make the consignment available, and prevents unnecessary ill feeling being created when the invoice arrives.

If a job is pre-booked for a certain collection time and the courier happens to arrive early, you should obviously make a charge for any waiting which starts before the pre-booked time has passed. Keeping your couriers aware that the job is pre-booked should avoid this possible source of confusion.

Absolute honesty on everyone's part is obviously a factor here as experience suggests that customers also keep an eye on how long couriers wait in their reception and will, quite rightly, refuse to pay the charges if they are incorrect.

Tony's Guide

to the courier industry

With this in mind you must impress upon your couriers the necessity of making a note of their arrival time, departure time and the reason for the waiting (if known), on their POD sheet, to provide your customers with the highest standards of accountability and service possible within the industry and this detail is crucial in justifying the charge.

So make it clear to your couriers that in order to make a claim for waiting/loading time they must be able to inform you of:

- ❑ the length of time they were waiting, together with the times between which the waiting/loading occurred

- ❑ where the waiting/loading occurred

- ❑ reason for the delay, if known.

The numeric value of the waiting / loading time to be added has a special field where it should be entered on each docket. The other information can be entered in a diary, or onto the booking notes feature on MTvan.com, providing an archive to which you can refer in the event of a later invoice query.

An example of an entry might be as follows:

"Courier waited 17 minutes at customers address (consignment still being photo-copied and wrapped), a further 20 at Liverpool (while documents were examined and signed) and a further 30 at delivery point (waiting for consignee to come back from lunch to sign for consignment) as our instructions were to deliver to Mr Brown only. This comes to a total of 67 minutes"

This example demonstrates the principle of keeping good notes, and no customer presented with this breakdown of the waiting time charge on their job could fail to be impressed by your efficiency and attention to detail. They will be far more likely to pass the job for immediate payment, than if all you can tell them was that your courier waited 67 minutes "somewhere, I think it was at more than one place" during the job. It is worth remembering that the invoice query may come two months after the job was completed.

It can often be a good idea to alert a customer of waiting/loading time charges being incurred *at the time at which the courier is waiting/loading*. This is not only for the reason of good customer care in keeping the customer well informed, but also so that they can verify the facts for themselves. This will again assist in preventing a possible dispute later on.

❏ Loading time

The idea here is to compensate company and courier for the amount of "lost" time incurred during loading and unloading. A job might involve carrying 30 large boxes, one by one, from a first floor customers address down to the couriers van - involving at least 60 trips up and down the stairs.

As with waiting time the loading or unloading of a van is not usually worth charging 15 minutes.

The detailing of the reasons for loading time charges should be recorded with just as much vigilance as with waiting time.

You cannot add waiting/loading time after the job has been invoiced and it is the courier's responsibility to remind you to add it to a job in good time. You can also ask couriers if they have any to be added before this occurs if you have time.

There are some special circumstances in which it is appropriate to waive these charges altogether, usually because you are charging plenty for the job already and any extra charges would be unreasonable. This is obviously for you to decide.

Tony's Guide
to the courier industry

❏ **Payment**

When you take a booking from someone who doesn't have an account with you, and you don't want to risk on giving them one immediately, you can offer them payment by cash, credit card, or cheque.

We strongly recommend the use of credit cards, as it avoids the inconvenience of handling cash or cheques. You do, however have to be alert for card fraud.

If you don't have a merchant account to enable you to take credit cards, MTvan.com can help you with this by offering settlement of the debt on the website (see FAQs on MTvan.com).

You can send a company VAT receipt with the courier if they are in the office at the time the booking is made, or you can post one at a later date. Explain to the caller if the receipt is going to be posted as this can help when the courier arrives to collect the cash, as sometimes people are unwilling to part with the payment without having the receipt in exchange.

❏ **Converting cash jobs into account jobs:**

Another way of handling a query from a caller who does not currently have an account and offers to pay cash, is to offer to open an account for them instantly and to invoice them for the job instead. After all, this is pretty much what you'd do if you had approached them in your role as salesman.

© Tim Gilbert 2005

Tony's Guide
to the courier industry

This is particularly recommended if the company is a large organisation or a Plc who say they might need you again in the future.

If it's a one-off job, you may as well get paid up front instead of waiting a minimum of 30 days for the money. So you need to ask questions to help you work out which applies to each caller.

If a caller without an account can be persuaded that they should go ahead with the booking on an account basis, here's a suggested procedure:

- ❏ Ask them to send the details of their first job in an email, or on a fax of their letterheaded notepaper, with all the usual information you require when taking a booking.

- ❏ Make sure they realise you need to receive the above before you will despatch the van.

- ❏ Ensure also that during this first conversation you say something like the following: "Although we are of course happy to do this first job for you without much formality, we will be posting you an Account Application/Conditions of Carriage form which needs to be fully completed, signed and returned to our head office so that a full credit account can be opened for you."

- ❏ When the email or fax arrives, get a courier to copy down the details from the fax, so that the job gets under way as soon as possible.

- ❏ Enter the job on the newly established account code

from the details on the fax.

- ❑ Send an Application form off to them first class or get the courier to drop it off when he collects, along with a brief covering letter which explains its purpose

- ❑ Send an introductory information pack thanking the customer for booking the first job and welcoming them aboard - the Application form can be enclosed with this if it does not go with the courier.

- ❑ Keep their faxed letterhead until you have been paid, as it may strengthen your case that binding contract existed to purchase the services which it describes.

- ❑ Decide whether they are a large account who intend to spend a lot quickly and whose credit-worthiness therefore needs checking out immediately. If so, use an on-line credit reference agency.

- ❑ Make an appointment to go and see them, to see what sales opportunities exist.

Summary:

Good controlling involves keeping service quality standards high by getting the most out of all your available resources to the benefit of all concerned.

Tony's Guide

to the courier industry

Tony's Guide

to the courier industry

❑ Purpose

You should aim to make your invoices perfect, as this will impress your customers, which will in turn lead to growth through recommendations. It will also limit the occurrence of credit notes and invoice and rider pay queries to the absolute minimum level possible and provide ideal conditions for early payment too.

Perfect data entered at the booking stage is your starting point, but given that things often change after a booking has been confirmed the data needs to be subsequently checked and corrected.

You can check yesterday's bookings first thing every day, to check that they are complete and accurate. This will make a huge difference to the quality of your invoices.

© Tim Gilbert 2005

Tony's Guide

to the courier industry

How your courier business might work financially   50

This section may help you when planning your courier business with your professional advisors. You'll need a cash flow forecast at the outset, however tedious this may seem. As with any business, there's no point in going to a lot of expense of time effort and money to set your courier business up, without being reasonably certain that you have enough cash available to run it.

You need to be sure that you can pay your bills as they arise, without necessarily having to wait to be paid in full by your customer. A cash flow forecast will show you how much spare cash you need to survive.

If you're a director of a limited company, you have a legal obligation to be reasonably sure that your business has the cash it needs to meet its obligations as they arise. A cash flow forecast is the first step. Ask your accountant to help you.

The following timetable of job-done-to-cash-collected, with bills paid along the way, is the one followed by courier companies who use MTvan.com's administration services, and it shows how important it is to have discipline in your invoicing and cash collection methods. It also shows how important it is to have enough funding available, if you are not going to just run out of cash before you are paid by your customer.

© Tim Gilbert 2005

- ❏ Job is booked by your customer in month One.

- ❏ This job is booked on MTvan.com and invoiced weekly. The invoice is produced by MTvan.com in the name of your business (this appears prominently on the invoice).

- ❏ The invoice is discreetly assigned (similarly to the way it would be to a factoring company) to MTvan.com.

- ❏ The courier is paid by you weekly, from figures provided by MTvan.com.

- ❏ The amount to be paid to each courier (according to your percentage pay rates) will be notified to you on pay advices which will be emailed from MTvan.com on the Wednesday following the week in which the work was done. (Work weeks run from Saturday to Friday).

- ❏ Within three weeks of the invoice date, MTvan.com pays to your business the amount invoiced, less the service charge.

- ❏ You should exercise a strict 30 days credit policy so the payment from the customer should arrive during month Three at the latest. MTvan.com takes credit controlling action during Month Two.

- ❏ You pay your trade creditors, usually in the month following the job.

- ❏ Operational costs also need to be paid and should be included in the model in the current month.

Tony's Guide

These figures, which you should check for yourself, may help your accountant prepare a budget and cash flow for you.

- ❏ Salaries   One employee in years 1 and 2.

- ❏ Salaries   Two employees in years 3 onwards.

- ❏ Salary cost   £230 per week plus NI.

- ❏ Vehicle costs   £100 per week.

- ❏ Telephone costs   1.25% of sales.

- ❏ Mobile phone costs   1.00% of sales.

- ❏ Postage, Packing and Stationery   £15 per week.

- ❏ Rent and Rates   £100 per week.

- ❏ Light and Heat   £15 per week.

- ❏ Repairs and renewals   £10 per week.

- ❏ Insurance   £10 per week.

- ❏ Professional charges   £20 per week.

© Tim Gilbert 2005

Tony's Guide
to the courier industry

- ☐ Computer charges   £20 per week.

- ☐ Uniform   £10 per week.

- ☐ Sales Literature   £5 per week.

- ☐ Stationery   £5 per week.

- ☐ Miscellaneous   £15 per week.

"I don't want to do business with those who don't make a profit, because they can't give the best service".

(Lee Bristol)

Tony's Guide

❑ **Assumptions**

We make the following assumptions for you to model, probably with the help of your accountant. It is important to remember that the costs of overheads will vary considerably in different areas and with variance in local and personal circumstances. You will need to undertake full research into all costs when preparing a business plan. Your accountant will be able to help with this.

Don't feel obliged to take on offices and staff too early in your plan. A lot of MTvan Members are doing very nicely running their business from their van and from their spare bedroom.

It should be noted that only the following figures are for example Profit and Loss and cash flow forecasts only and should not be taken as an indication of actual results achievable. Ask your accountant.

❑ **Sales growth**

Sales growth has been assumed from actual sales growth of typical courier businesses.

This growth is linear for modelling purposes. The previously achieved sales growth curves do stray from this.

❑ Cost of Sales

Cost of sales is usually 50 - 70% for same day courier work. Because the couriers are paid a percentage of the amount charged, this is easy to calculate and monitor.

❑ Example Budget and Cash flow

MTvan.com can provide you with an Excel file example budget and cash flow. See our website for details of prices, or call MTvan.com on 01480 309347.

When you have prepared your cash flow forecast, you will be in a position to know whether you have sufficient cash to be able to meet your commitments as they arise, before you receive payment from your customers. If there is a shortfall, you'll need to make arrangements in advance to be able to borrow enough to keep you going.

Many courier companies factor their debts. This means that they get most of the value of their sales invoices paid to them instantly, which improves their cash flow. Ask your accountant what this means for your courier business, but be cautious about accepting the first offer of factoring which comes your way.

MTvan.com can pay you for your invoices, then collect the money from your customers. Call Tim on 01480 309347 for details.

Tony's Guide

Monthly, you should be able to produce for yourself, the following information. MTvan.com can do this for you. It's very important to stay in touch with the way your figures are going, to allow to you take action if things are going wrong.

Most directors of failed companies blame "lack of up to date accurate financial information" for their inability to save their company. In other words, they didn't even know they were about to hit the rocks. To prevent this happening to you, you need the following information on a regular basis:

"If you don't drive your business you will be driven out of business".

(B. C. Forbes)

- ❏ Your sales for the previous month.

- ❏ Your output VAT for the previous month.

- ❏ Details of customers who have paid.

- ❏ Details of advances made by MTvan.com to you.

- ❏ Details of customers whose accounts are overdue and/or on stop.

- ❏ Details of deductions made in respect of customers who have not paid in time.

- ❏ Details of deductions made in respect of MTvan.com's Service Charge.

- ❏ Details of the net payment to be made by MTvan.com to you.

- ❏ Details of customers who are considered to be "bad debts", and reasons for this, and details of action taken to date to recover the debt.

❑ **Preparing the data for invoicing**

Most people who use your business will accept one invoice per week. These invoices are referred to by the month in which they were raised and are often regarded as one single invoice.

The options which you should make available to your customer are:

❑ One invoice per job, for customers with various departments and authorisation, but with little usage.

❑ One invoice per week: this should be the default setting for new accounts. You should invoice weekly and chase the money very promptly until you get the results of your credit check.

Tony's Guide

to the courier industry

Investing in a computer system to run your business   55

You will need a computer to run your courier business, preferably connected by broadband to the internet.

You can do this for just a few hundred pounds from your local computer shop, or see MTvan.com "Deals and Discounts" section, or from eBay.

We suggest that you do not rush into investing in a "system" or special software to run your courier business. Most of what you need to do in the early days can be done perfectly well on the standard Microsoft Office programs that come with a pc. Letters can be done on Word. Invoices can be done on Excel using the Excel invoice templates. Lists of couriers, customers, and sales prospects can be kept on Outlook.

When the time comes, and if you really feel you want to invest some money, there are various systems on offer such as CourierSystems and Freedom, as well as the pc-based system offered by MTvan.com.

You can use MTvan's pc-based system for your invoicing and full sales ledger administration. This means that you can enter bookings onto your own private MTvan system on your pc, send jobs to MTvan.com to get bids where necessary, and then invoice the work on your pc without further effort.

If you want, MTvan.com can also chase and collect the money for you, and advance you the money before your customer has paid.

© Tim Gilbert 2005

Tony's Guide

We suggest that you contact MTvan.com to discuss these options before making your final decision, on 01480 309347.

Investing in premises

56

Like all costs associated with running a courier business, taking on premises should be put off for as long as possible.

For as long as is practical, there's nothing to be ashamed of in running it all from your spare bedroom. After all, to start with, you're running a sales operation from your mobile phone, so as long as you have room for a pc, you'll be in business at very low cost.

As your courier business grows, pressure will mount from neighbours, spouses, landlords and so on, requiring you to move into somewhere more sensibly business-like.

Keep it cheap in the early days. If you know of anyone already running any kind of business, especially one using couriers, you may be able to share a few square feet of their premises to start off with.

Failing that, try the local council. They often have "business start-up" units available at very low rents, for the good of the local economy. These also have the advantage usually of being let on "easy in easy out" terms. This is important, as it keeps your options wide open for the future.

Get office furniture and equipment from eBay, or from local auctions, to keep the cost to a minimum.

Tony's Guide

to the courier industry

Staff pay policy

57

Your business should be an equal opportunities employer, and you have a legal obligation to ensure that the equal opportunities policy is actually adhered to.

You should have a pay-scale exists for every operational post within your courier office, which you should adhere to when engaging new staff.

This adherence is important, to prevent pay "leap-frogging" as comparisons between pay levels between staff are inevitable, and it can be very destructive if wide and unjustifiable differentials are discovered.

Most importantly, a policy can protect you from accidental discrimination between one employee and another. You should consult your solicitor about this.

You can find out more about the issues you'll face when you employ people on the Business Link website:

www.businesslink.gov.uk/employreg/

"First-rate people hire first-rate people; second-rate people hire third-rate people."
(Leo Rosten)

Tony's Guide

to the courier industry

Tony's Guide

to the courier industry

58

As a general rule your courier business should pay to the courier 50-70% of the charge to the customer, to keep you competitive with the rest of the industry.

Individual and local exceptions can be made, but it has been found that paying too little damages courier relations, and paying too much is not sustainable financially. Above all, it is important to pay what you have agreed to pay, or your reputation will suffer.

If it is not viable for you or for the courier to pay 50 - 70%, you need to raise your prices, or find another customer.

Tony's Guide

to the courier industry

Tony's Guide
to the courier industry

Staff pay policy**59**

A Contract of Employment should be used for every employee, which you should obtain from your solicitor.

Before you start employing people, you should read up on the Employment Protection Act and other employment legislation. Your accountant can help you with this.

© Tim Gilbert 2005

Tony's Guide

to the courier industry

Tony's Guide

to the courier industry

Keeping your books and records in order   60

You should get yourself professional advice about record keeping at an early stage in your business. You should start with an accountant. Don't be pushed into anything complicated or expensive to start with.

You should also check the "Starting a business" sections at www.inlandrevenue.gov.uk and at www.customs.gov.uk

Generally, though, something simple in the way of keeping records as you go along is all you need. You can leave the boring business of "producing monthly accounts" and "doing the VAT" to your accountant. You'll need the accounts to show your bank manager, and to keep in touch with how your business is progressing.

The areas you really need concentrate on are:

❑ prompt invoicing and effective credit controlling, so you don't run out of cash

❑ accurate payment of your couriers, so you don't run out of couriers.

MTvan.com can help you with both of these areas from the outset, with systems to make this easier.

Tony's Guide

to the courier industry

Sample credit controlling timetable

You need a plan to ensure that you collect money owed to you on time.

Here is the timetable that MTvan.com uses, for courier companies who use their administration services. The timetable may be useful if you are planning to do your own administration:

30 - 35 days

MTvan.com sends a *reminder fax* to your customer which politely says that their account is now slightly overdue. This simply jolts the memory of most customers and we expect payment shortly after. In many cases, this fax is followed by a phone call, checking that they have received the invoice, and that it is in order.

37 - 42 days

MTvan.com sends an *overdue fax* which points out that we have already reminded them once and that their account will be stopped in seven days if they have not paid by then. In most cases, this fax is followed by a phone call to remind them to pay.

At this point MTvan.com emails you the "Stop List" for your customers a, which gives details of those accounts from which a cheque needs to be collected. The list appears as follows giving the details of the account code, the account name and the amount overdue which must be collected immediately for the account to stay open. The list looks like:

From paul Wed Aug 7 14:17:34 2003
From: "Paul (credit control)" <creditcontrol@MTvan.com>
To: adriana@bigspender.com,
Subject: Overdue List-004
Date: Wed, 7 Aug 03 14:17:33 GMT

07/08/03

These accounts will go on STOP 7 days after the date of this report,
if they fail to pay.

ACCOUNT CODE	NAME	OS BALANCE
4MATRI	CITRIX TECHNOLOGY LIMITED	112.40
4ERICA	SMILES ASSOCIATES	140.72
4ADVAN	ADVANCE LTD	75.20

44 - 49 days

The debt is now over a fortnight overdue and MTvan.com sends out a *stop letter*, which makes them aware that should they try and book any more work with us, they will be refused credit facilities

At this stage you should either collect cheque for the outstanding amount or be certain that there is a cheque in the post. MTvan.com has many years' experience of credit control. It is usually easy to tell trustworthy people at this stage; if someone has really written a cheque they can remember the details. It helps you as a business to have as many active accounts as possible, so if you have a courier nearby and can cheaply ensure that you have a cheque collected, it is worth paying one of your drivers a nominal amount for going slightly out of his way to collect it.

Notify your credit control of any details to do with any account from the stop list, eg if you have collected a cheque, or (nightmare) if their premises are suddenly empty.

50 to 90 days

If the account is still not settled at around 60 days, MTvan.com send all remaining unqueried debts to a cash collection agency. This agency sends two letters and make calls. Any queries are referred to us and we deal with them in the normal way.

If there are no genuine problems or queries over the next two weeks the cash collection agency obtains legal authority from us to issue a court summons to collect the debt.

We will do everything we can to avoid you having to appear as a witness in court and lose out on an extra day growing the business.

Any invoices or debts that drop out of the above system through unresolved queries must be dealt with as quickly as possible so that we have enough time to start legal proceedings and have some sort of outcome by the time the debt is four months old.

Tony's Guide

to the courier industry

When an invoice is still unpaid, despite everything, on day 90, MTvan.com hands the debt back to your business. This unpaid amount will usually take the form of a deduction from the payment by MTvan.com to your business.

MTvan.com will give you an up to date report on where our chasing has led to, whether bailiffs have been instructed to collect the cash, and it will be up to you to chase the money at this stage.

If however you would like MTvan.com to continue to chase the money on your behalf, this is also possible.

At this point, it is worth visiting the business concerned, to discuss face to face the reason for non-payment and to help you decide on your next move.

Once any genuine reasons for non-payment are removed, there is a lot you can achieve by exerting gentle pressure in the form of making yourself more of a pain unpaid than paid. Something as simple as turning up and waiting in reception for a cheque, with immaculate manners of course, can often make all the difference.

If all else fails, you will have to consult your solicitor about your legal options in recovering your money.

Summary

From all of this, you can see that collecting the money for courier work done is a job in itself. It's one which is often neglected

© Tim Gilbert 2005

"because I'm too busy doing everything else". But if you run out of cash, you don't have anything to be busy doing, as your business will be bust.

So we recommend having a solid plan in place, from the outset, to allocate enough time and effort to invoicing and credit controlling.

Tony's Guide

By now, you should have lots of ideas on how to become a courier, and how to set up and run a courier business of your own.

We wish you every success with your venture, and look forward to meeting you on the internet in the very near future.

The following sections contain further information and "Frequently Asked Questions" which may be useful to you.

Tony's Guide

"Many of life's failures are people who did not realise how close they were to success when they gave up." (Thomas Edison)

Tony's Guide
to the courier industry

MTvan.com is a website for couriers and courier companies, with 100's of "courier members", and some really useful "end user" customers. The customers get their work covered by the courier members, who also trade work between themselves.

What it's good for rather depends on who you are.

If you're a courier looking for work to fill your empty van, it's a network of contacts and opportunities, and it's a source of work. Whether you're just starting out in the business as an owner-driver courier, or an old hand with years of experience behind you, MTvan.com gives you instant access to people who have goods to move.

If you're a courier company looking for a courier to cover your overflow work, it's a source of couriers throughout the UK. This enables you to say "yes" to a much broader range of requests from your customers, knowing you have access to couriers in numbers normally only previously available to really huge couriers companies.

Whoever you are, it can even do your invoicing and other courier administration, leaving you free to get on with running your courier operation.

And it's a networking opportunity for everyone to make new contacts in the courier industry. Contacts are always useful, whether you're seeking advice, couriers, customers, premises, vehicles, staff, or even a buyer for your business.

© Tim Gilbert 2005

Tony's Guide
to the courier industry

Bookings are shown on this page in "closest to you" order. So the nearest jobs to you are at the top. If you want to find a job close to somewhere else, just enter the town name in the box and click on "Search"

You can find 100's of couriers and courier companies around the UK using "Find a Courier"

When you've completed a job, you can enter the POD here on MTvan

You can let other courier members know where you are during the day with TxtMeMT

You can bid a price on any job showing in white or light blue

To bid, just click on the job reference

There are no rules on how much to bid. Just bid the best price you are happy to do the job for.

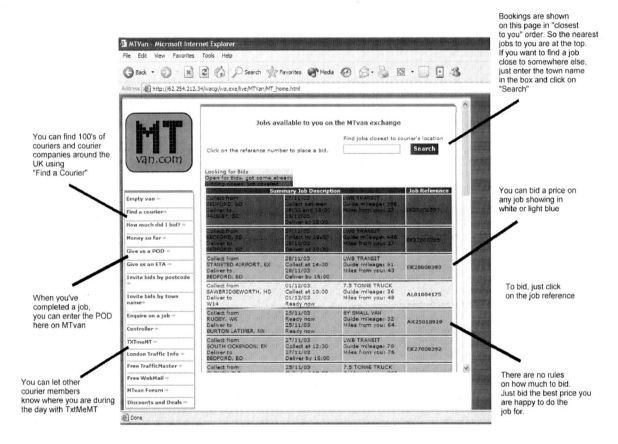

Tony's Guide

Well, let's start with "what's the problem?". There's more courier work out there than you get to know about, and you're running an empty van more often than makes sense.

Even the odd extra job here and there would make a lot of difference.

MTvan.com can help you. When you sign up, you're joining a community of over 2000 members, many of them courier companies looking for reliable owner drivers to cover their work.

So there are lots of new contacts to be made, and there's quality courier work to bid for.

And if you tell MTvan.com where you're based and where you're heading, we'll match up this information with the courier work on offer, and we'll send you instant text alerts with details of courier work which may be of interest to you. You can bid for any work which suits your route.

There are no fixed rules on what to bid; just offer the best price you're happy to do the job for, and a sensible, honest pickup time. You can add comments to your bid, such as "experienced MTvan member" or "leaving Birmingham in 30 minutes" if you think it will help.

And controllers all over the UK know where you are and where you'll be empty, so they can call you direct.

© Tim Gilbert 2005

Tony's Guide
to the courier industry

MTvan.com has the biggest membership of its kind, it's growing every day, and it's the future way of working as an owner-driver.

Tony's Guide

to the courier industry

Welcome to Alpha TransLogistics (ATL).

Owner Driver offering courier and small removal services

The Driver: Experienced in driving in the UK and in Europe. Bilingual German English. Reliable. Smart appearance.

The Van: Late plate Fiat Ducato Maxi 14 (LWB, HR), payload approx. 1.5 tons.

The Insurance: Van - Norwich Union + GIT up to £10,000 by Kerwin Smith

The Services: Sameday and Next Day - Door to Door

24 hours 7 days per week dedicated vehicle service. Driver collects and hand delivers. POD. Coverage: UK & Europe.

MTvan Find a Courier Details:
MICHAEL JAKOB-WHITWORTH
User : W334
PENRITH, CU
Postcode: CA10 1TN
Tel: 01768362100
Mob: 07989120344

Empty van ⇒

Find a courier ⇒

How much did I bid? ⇒

Money so far ⇒

Give us a POD ⇒

Give us an ETA ⇒

Invite bids by postcode ⇒

Invite bids by town name ⇒

Enquire on a job ⇒

Controller ⇒

TXTmeMT ⇒

London Traffic Info ⇒

Free TrafficMaster ⇒

Free WebMail ⇒

MTvan Forum ⇒

Discounts and Deals ⇒

Logout

Frequently Asked Questions | Contact Us | Terms and Conditions | Feedback | © MTvan 2002.

Tony's Guide

to the courier industry

Tony's Guide

MTvan.com has courier work available all over the UK.

There are two sorts of work.

There is lots of work available from Courier Companies.

There is also the work available from MTvan.com's own managed accounts.

Both appear on our courier work exchange page "Empty Van".

If you see a job you want on the Empty Van page, you can bid for it, and the controller will call you to accept your bid. From then on, it's between the two of you.

If there's a phone number in the job's "Comments" box, you can bid by phone.

Or you can bid on the internet on your pc.

Or you can bid from your van if you have an O2 XDA II smartphone, an IPAQ, an Orange P900 phone or similar. Just log on from your van, find the job nearest to you, and bid for it.

If you're out on the road, you can ask to be notified by instant text message of any jobs in your area. Just click on "TxtMeJobs" in the TxtMeMT area.

© Tim Gilbert 2005

Tony's Guide

to the courier industry

Of course, if you have courier work you need covered, you too can offer it for bids.

Tony's Guide

Courier companies who have a job they want covered simply click on the "Invite Bids" link. They enter the details by entering the two postcodes...

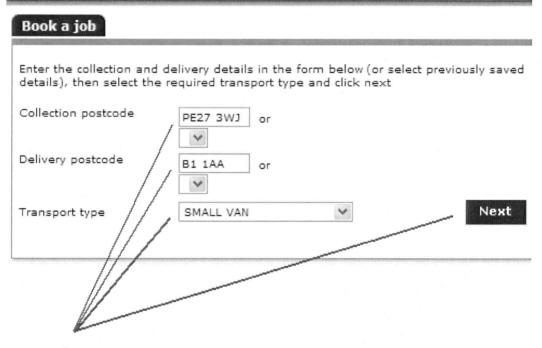

Book a job

Enter the collection and delivery details in the form below (or select previously saved details), then select the required transport type and click next

Collection postcode   PE27 3WJ   or

Delivery postcode   B1 1AA   or

Transport type   SMALL VAN   Next

Enter two postcodes and vehicle type, and click next

Tony's Guide

to the courier industry

...then completing the details, and clicking on submit...

Book a job

Please check the information below. We require everything marked with an asterisk (*)

Customer order ref	XYZ123	*
Booked by	CALLER'S NAME	*
Recipients mobile		(no spaces)
Guide mileage	101	
Guide price £	0.00	
Comments	PH BIDS 07976746191. 1 PALLET. 20 KGS	

Put your phone number here if you want bids by phone

(eg: if you want bidders to phone you, you may enter your phone number here.)

Collection details			Delivery details	
PICKUP LTD	*	Building name/number	DROP LTD	*
Stephenson Road		Address	1 ACACIA AVE	
			Central Birmingham	
St. Ives			Birmingham	
Cambridgeshire		County		
PE27 3WJ		Postcode	B1 1AA	
7 / 6 / 2004		Date	7 / 6 / 2004	
Ready Now		Time type	By time entered below	
14 : 49		Required time (24 hour)	18 : 00	
:		End time (24 hour)	:	

Enter the details circled, click "submit", and that's it

If this is a regular job why not
Save collection details ⇒
Save delivery details ⇒
Save all details ⇒

Submit **Back**

...A summary of these details will appear on the Empty Van exchange page, coloured white, for you to bid on:

Tony's Guide
to the courier industry

Jobs available to you on the MTvan exchange

Find jobs closest to courier's location

Click on the reference number to place a bid.

[Search]

Looking for Bids
Open for Bids, got some already
Bidding closed, job covered

Click on these links to bid

Summary Job Description			Job Reference
Collect from WARWICK, WK Deliver to PRESCOT, MS	09/06/04 Ready now 09/06/04 ASAP	7.5 TONNE TRUCK Guide mileage: 121 Miles from you:	AF09103413
Collect from SOUTHAM, WK Deliver to YEADON, WY	11/06/04 Collect after 13:00 11/06/04 ASAP	7.5 TONNE TRUCK Guide mileage: 143 Miles from you: 11	AF11000746
Collect from NE625HE Deliver to PAISLEY	09/06/04 Collect at 09:00 09/06/04 ASAP	By Small Van Guide mileage: 156 Miles from you: 13	AF09004412
Collect from COVENTRY CV6 Deliver to COVENTRY CV2	09/06/04 Ready now 09/06/04 ASAP	Guide mileage: 4 Miles from you: 14	AF09008902
Collect from COVENTRY CV2 Deliver to	09/06/04 Ready now 09/06/04	Guide mileage: 33 Miles from you: 16	AF09008903

As soon as this happens, details of the job are texted and emailed to any Members based or empty in the area.

Courier companies who are happy to receive bids by phone, put their phone number in the "Comments" box. If there is a phone number there, feel free to bid by phone. Just work out the best price you are happy to do the job for, and a sensible and honest pick-up time, and then phone the number on the job.

Or you can bid for the job by clicking on the link as shown above, offering you a price and a time. The job will then turn light blue. Jobs are left open for bids until enough bids have been received or the job is covered.

If yours is the winning bid, the controller will in touch with you directly and give you details of the job, and will allocate the job to you as the successful bidder. This will turn the job dark blue, so everyone knows that bidding is closed.

It will also enable you as the successful bidder to log and download a POD sheet, if this makes sense. To download a POD sheet, just go into "Give us an ETA" or "Give us a POD", click on the job reference number, and click "OK to Print". Only you, as the successful bidder, will be able to do this.

Later you'll be able to log in and enter the POD details (name and time), using "Give us a POD".

If you see a job you want to bid on, simply click on the job reference number on the right, and enter your bid details. Just work out the best price you are happy to do the job for, and how long it will take you to collect, and enter these details in the bid page.

If there's a phone number in the Comments box, you can bid there and then on the phone. Just work out the best price you are happy to do the job for, and a sensible and honest pick-up time, and phone the number on the job.

Keep an eye on the job on the Empty Van page. When the job goes dark blue, if you haven't heard that you were successful, you know you didn't get the job. If yours is the successful bid, the controller will

Tony's Guide
to the courier industry

call you, and having agreed everything with you, will allocate the job to you. This will allow you to log on to MTvan.com to download a paper POD sheet (click on the job number in "Give us a POD"), and then later to enter the POD (Proof of Delivery) details.

If the job is for one of MTvan.com's managed accounts, you will be paid direct by MTvan.com within a few weeks. If the job is from another Member, they will pay you direct. Do be sure that you discuss your payment terms when taking on any job.

© Tim Gilbert 2005

Tony's Guide

to the courier industry

Tony's Guide
to the courier industry

MTvan.com offers you work from some of the best customers in the country.

Once you've got some work, "Give us a POD" allows you to enter the POD data straight onto the booking.

Obviously we can't pay you until you've delivered the job and entered a POD onto MTvan.com. There are three ways to do this:

From your home or office computer on MTvan.com, using the "Give us a POD" button.

From your van, using an XDA or Sony mobile computer, or a PC tablet, to connect instantly to MTvan.com, and using the "Give us a POD" button.

From your Mobile Phone using Text Messaging. It's really easy, quick and cheap and you can do it as soon as you've delivered your package.

This is what you do:

On your Mobile Phone type -nnnnnn#1#mmmm

eg -123456#1#SMITH
ie -[job reference]#[number of items]#[Name of person who received it]

Then text this info in this format to 07973 748159

© Tim Gilbert 2005

Tony's Guide
to the courier industry

If you are one of the many courier businesses already signed up to MTvan.com to give us your POD's, and you'd like to use more of the features as described here, please discuss this with your usual contact, or email Tony Burdon info@mtvan.com

Our Members' Hotline is 01948 667371.

Tony's Guide

to the courier industry

As well as using MTvan.com to give your courier business national courier coverage, you can also use MTvan's pc-based software to invoice your customers.

It's all based on your own pc, so you know you are keeping your own information completely private.

It's simple, secure, and has gives you all the features of the MTvan courier work exchange together with invoicing at the click of a mouse.

We can give you a demonstration without obligation.

Please email tim@mtvan.com if you want to know more, or call Tim on 01480 309347.

© Tim Gilbert 2005

Tony's Guide

to the courier industry

Tony's Guide
to the courier industry

If you're thinking about becoming a courier, MTvan.com can help you.

To get started, you'll need to get yourself properly equipped and insured, and you'll need to start making the right contacts to get yourself some courier work. If you're really serious about doing things properly, joining MTvan.com is an ideal way to start.

When you join MTvan.com, we'll send you free copy of "Tony's Guide to the Courier Industry" (described as "The best courier manual available", and published by Trafford Press, usual price £14.99), which describes in detail what you need to do to get started properly, and how to avoid the pitfalls.

On the MTvan.com website, you'll find 100's of courier company contacts throughout the UK, a Forum where you can learn and exchange questions and ideas, and lots of features to put you in touch with people who have courier work in search of a courier.

If you're determined to get out of the office and succeed in this challenging and exciting industry, you've come to the right place.

Tony's Guide

to the courier industry

The quickest way to find the right courier is to Invite Bids on your job. You just Invite Bids, and people who want the job come to you to say they'd like to do the job, which is obviously quicker, easier and cheaper than phoning a whole list of people.

You can look Members' detail up on MTvan.com's courier directory, or use it to find couriers throughout the UK to cover your work. You can search by name or location. The list will give you contact details including phone numbers, so you can make fast contact with their control room.

Many Members have "Trusted Status", showing that other Members are happy to trust them with their work. Members with the most "Trusted Status" with other Members are shown at the top.

Members can also update their own details with their insurance cover and fleet size.

For maximum reassurance, use the "Track this Member" feature. This allows you, with the Member's permission, to track their position, so you can be as confident about giving a job to an MTvan Member as you can about giving one to your own fleet.

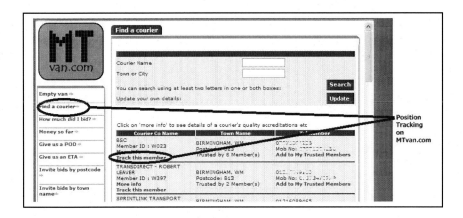

Tony's Guide
to the courier industry

We know how important it is to choose carefully when giving work to a courier. We select very carefully the couriers we use to cover our managed account courier work.

We have a set of established supplier and sub-contractor relationships, as anyone would expect.

These suppliers are our "Trusted Members" on MTvan.com

This has given us fantastic reach across the UK to manage these national contracts who demand collections from anywhere at the drop of a hat, 24/7.

Obviously, there are important issues of quality. We can't just pick "any old Tom Dick or Harry" to cover this important work.

So we use a system of strict approvals here, which works as follows:

You are "ready-approved" if:

* We have given you work successfully in the past.
or
* You have been recommended to us by someone in the trade we know and can trust.
or
* You have been previously approved by one of our customers.

You can become "approved" if you:

Tony's Guide

to the courier industry

* Are a member of MTvan.com
and
* You have expressed an interest in working for MTvan.com (eg you've bid on a job)
and
* You have faxed us proof of identity and address (VAT reg Certificate or utility bill)
and
* You have faxed us a Goods in Transit Insurance certificate
and
* You sound right on the phone
and
* Your price is right
and
* You'll accept self-billing
and
* There's no reason we know of not to use you.

It helps become approved if:

* You have a website of your own linked to the "Find a Courier" section in MTvan.com
or
* You have sent us a picture and other details for us to use on the Find a Courier pages.
or
* You can fax us a recent "Police check" form.
or
* You can fax us a copy of a recent valid ID badge of a major courier company.

Doing business this way works for us. We get no complaints from our customers about the quality of the couriers we use.

Tony's Guide
to the courier industry

Everyone in the courier industry builds a list of people they can trust to cover their work.

For many courier companies that means a list of their "own" couriers who they use all the time, and a second list of trusted subcontractors.

Courier Companies on MTvan.com do this by building their own lists of "Trusted Members" by selecting those Members they have come to trust, or who have been recommended.

When a Member asks you to become their Trusted Member, you will receive an email asking you to provide further details about yourself, which, if you click on the link in the email, will appear in your Find a Courier entry.

When a courier company is looking for a courier to cover a job, or when deciding whether to accept a bid from you, they can look at your listing and see how many other Members trust you. The higher the number, the more confident they can be that you are reliable.

Also, when you sign up for MTvan.com, you are asked if you hold a valid ID badge for any of the big courier companies listed there.

If you say yes, it'll appear with a tick against the relevant courier company name.

© Tim Gilbert 2005

Tony's Guide

to the courier industry

This gives further reassurance to anyone using you for the first time, that you have been checked by someone with quality standards.

It's worth asking everyone who has ever used you to offer you Trusted Member status, as the more you have, the higher up the list you will appear in "Find a Courier". Just phone them and ask them to add you to their Trusted Members on MTvan.com.

Tony's Guide

to the courier industry

Maximise your earnings by letting everyone know where you are during the day. Anyone looking for an empty van can look through the messages for anyone coming empty near their pick-up, and call you direct. Don't be out of touch just because you're out on the road.

To give yourself the best chance of extra work, use the "TxtMeJobs" feature on MTvan.com to get Instant Text Alerts of any jobs near your home town, near your "MT town" and near your route.

© Tim Gilbert 2005

Tony's Guide

to the courier industry

First go to the MTvan.com website

From your browser:

www.mtvan.com

Tony's Guide

to the courier industry

Logging in to MTvan.com

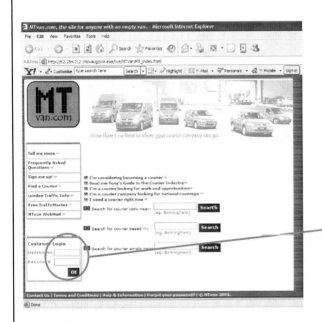

Login: <eg Z001 W001 X001>
Password: <your password>

...and Click OK

Inviting Bids on a job

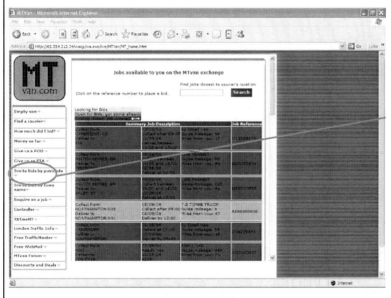

Click on "Invite Bids".

Tony's Guide

Inviting Bids on a job

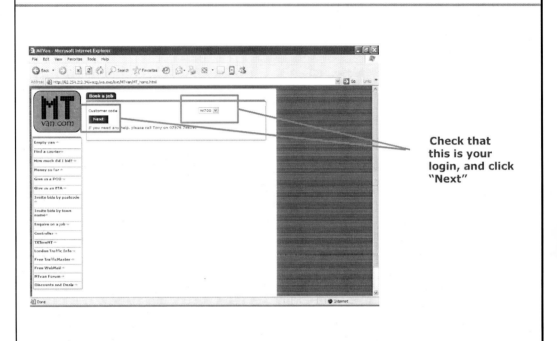

Check that this is your login, and click "Next"

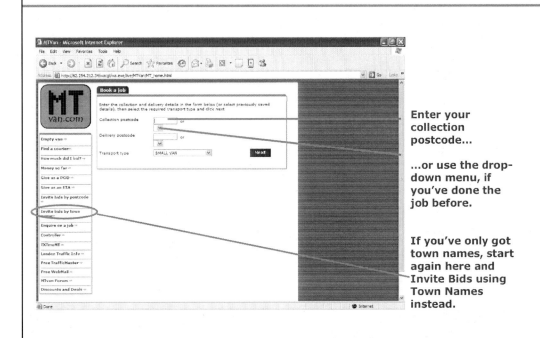

Collection details

Enter your collection postcode...

...or use the drop-down menu, if you've done the job before.

If you've only got town names, start again here and Invite Bids using Town Names instead.

Tony's Guide
to the courier industry

Delivery Postcode

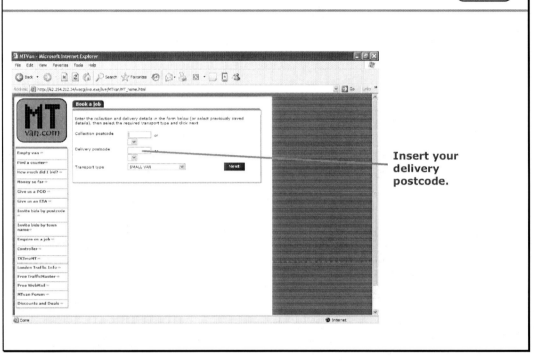

Insert your delivery postcode.

Tony's Guide

Service type (ie what sort of vehicle)

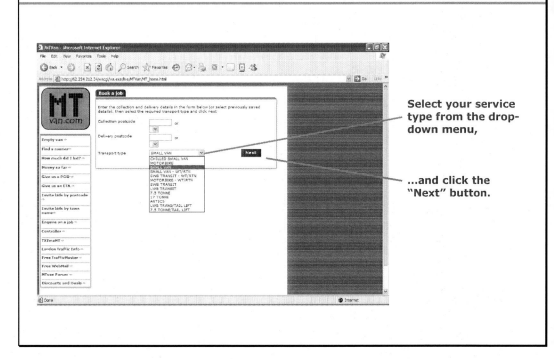

Select your service type from the drop-down menu,

...and click the "Next" button.

Tony's Guide
to the courier industry

Check the addresses and add references

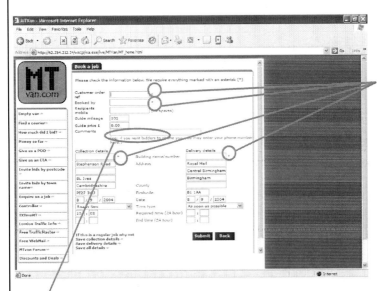

Most of the fields will fill automatically.

Fill in all the remaining job details. You must enter details in all the fields marked with an asterisk (*).

You can leave "Recipients mobile" blank.

"Customer Order Ref" is for your own order number if you have one, or just enter "none"

"Booked by" is your name.

If you want bidders to call you, you can enter your phone number here

Check you're happy with the job details

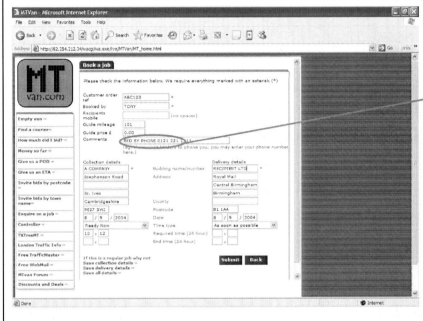

Your screen should now look like this.

You are welcome to use this area to give any information which will help bidders. Eg "two pallets total weight 200kg" or "Payment terms 30 days" or to give your company name if you think this helps.

Tony's Guide

to the courier industry

Entering the collection time

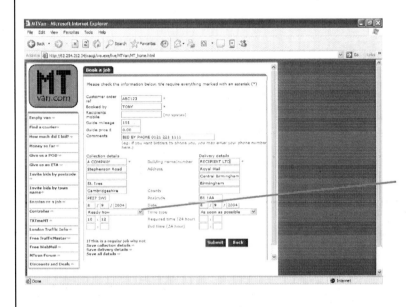

If it's just "collect asap", just leave it as "Ready Now"

Or, from the drop-down menu, select the collection option you require, and if necessary enter the collection time details in the boxes below.

Tony's Guide

to the courier industry

Entering the delivery time

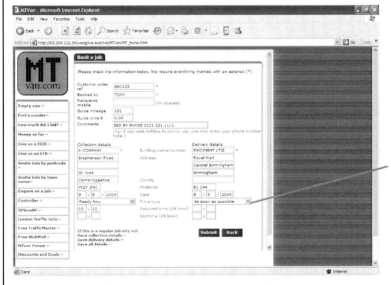

Repeat the same steps for the delivery option you require.

Tony's Guide

Saving details of regular jobs to save time later

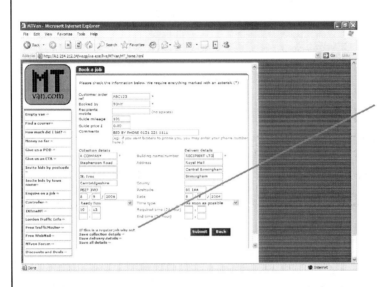

If this is a job that is frequently repeated,

...you can opt to save the details of the job.

This will save you time later, as you will then be able to use the drop-down's on the "Book a Job" screen.

Tony's Guide

to the courier industry

Submit the booking

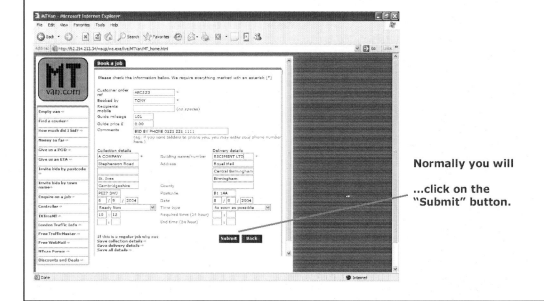

Normally you will

...click on the "Submit" button.

© Tim Gilbert 2005

Tony's Guide

Confirming the booking

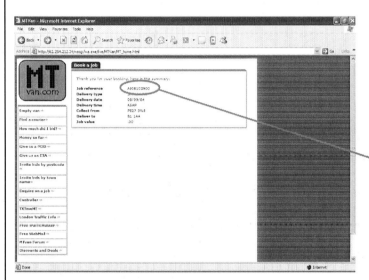

Your booking is confirmed when you see this confirmation screen.

This is the Job Number for your booking.

Tony's Guide

to the courier industry

Checking the booking on the MTvan exchange page

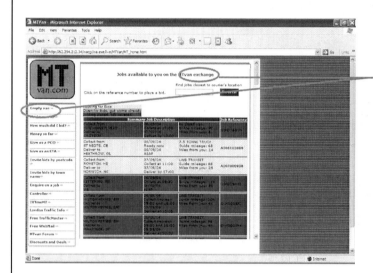

A summary of your booking will now appear on the MTvan exchange page, so that other Members can bid for it.

They appear in "closest to you at the top" order, so you may have to scroll down to find yours.

Check that it appears as you want it to, then wait for the bids to arrive on your mobile, and in your email.

Emails and text messages will be sent automatically to Members, to invite them to bid. All Members are welcome to bid.

Tony's Guide

to the courier industry

What to do with bids

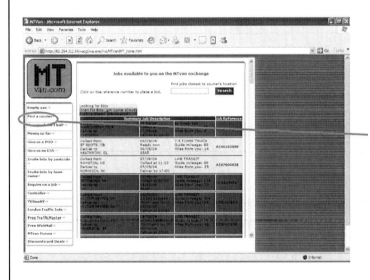

Bids will come as text messages to your mobile, and as emails, and as phone calls if you have put your phone number on the booking.

You are not obliged to accept any bid.

You can check out who each bidder is in "Find a Courier".

Look for insurance details, and a picture, and whether he/she is a "Trusted Member".

Once you have a shortlist, call them in the normal way.

Tony's Guide
to the courier industry

Once you've agreed everything with the successful bidder

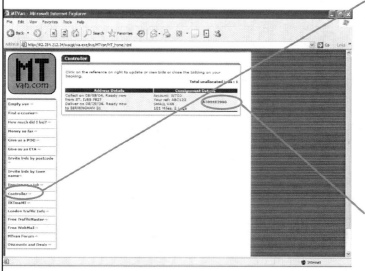

Click on "Controller" to go to your private control screen to find your bookings.

You now need to allocate the booking to the successful bidder.

This allows the successful bidder to see the FULL details of the booking for the first time, and to print a POD sheet if required, and later to enter a POD.

Click on the Reference to select the particular job

Tony's Guide

Once you've agreed everything with the successful bidder

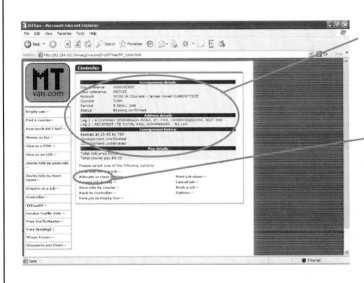

When you've clicked on the Reference, you will see the booking in more detail, together with a list of options below.

You can use any of the options, as required.

To allocate the booking to the successful bidder, click on "Allocate".

Also click on this option if you change your mind and want to close the bidding.

Tony's Guide

Once you've agreed everything with the successful bidder

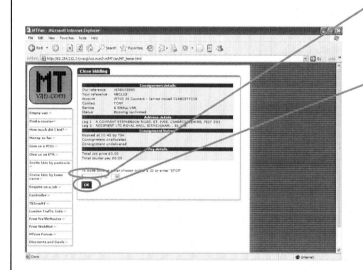

Enter the successful bidder's id here (eg Z001 or W700 etc).

If you just want to close the bidding, just enter "STOP" here.

Then click "OK".

By allocating the booking to the successful bidder, you close the bidding (the booking turns dark blue on the exchange page), and you allow the successful bidder to print a POD sheet if they need one.

Also, you can use the booking as a record to check the successful bidder's invoice later.

Tony's Guide

Enquiring on your job later

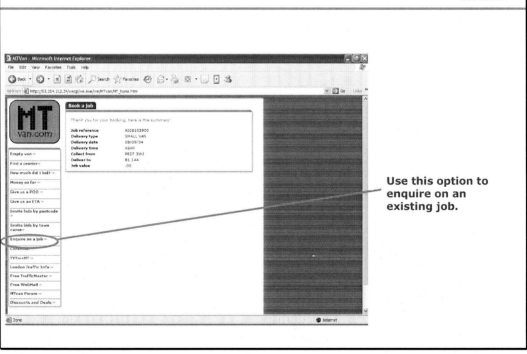

Use this option to enquire on an existing job.

Tony's Guide

Using a date range to enquire

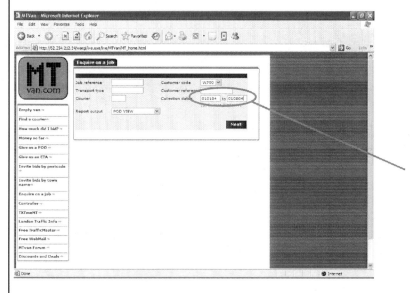

Enter the Reference of the job you are looking for,

...or it is sometimes simpler to enter a date range...

Tony's Guide

Checking on progress

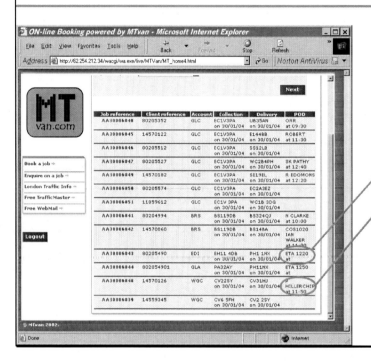

... and then browse the list to select the job you are looking for.

Jobs that have not yet been completed will have an ETA, if you've asked the successful bidder to enter one. (They just enter it in the "give us an ETA" option)

Completed jobs will have a POD, (entered by the successful bidder in the "Give us a POD" option), listing the name of the person who signed for it and the time at which it was delivered.

Tony's Guide

Looking for more details

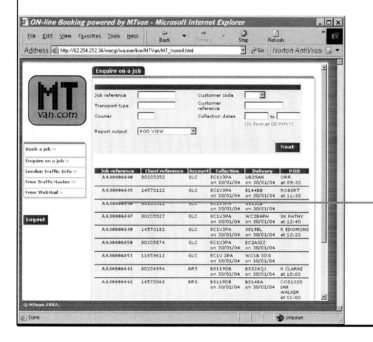

If you need more details, click on the job number.

Tony's Guide

Enquiring on completed job details

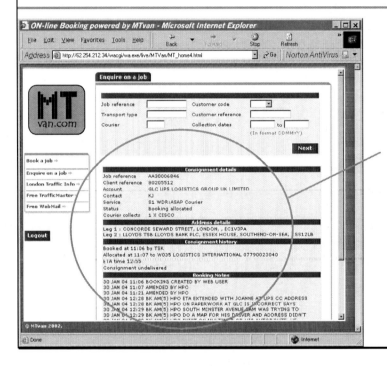

Further details and notes on the booking.

Tony's Guide
to the courier industry

How can I contact the Author of Tony's Guide?   77

You can email Tim Gilbert: tim@mtvan.com

FAQ: How do I know where postcodes are?   78

Here's a look up table of postcodes.

You can Invite a Bid by town name or by postcode.

We encourage the use of postcodes when inviting bids in the UK on MTvan.com, as they are more accurate than town names for the purpose of calculating guide mileages.

MTvan.com displays only the area, not the full postcode entered by you, so your confidentiality is preserved.

By Postcode		By Town	
AB	Aberdeen	Aberdeen	AB
AL	St Albans	Bath	BA
B	Birmingham	Belfast	BT
BA	Bath	Birmingham	B
BB	Blackburn	Blackburn	BB
BD	Bradford	Blackpool	FY
BH	Bournemouth	Bolton	BL
BL	Bolton	Bournemouth	BH

© Tim Gilbert 2005

BN	Brighton	Bradford	BD
BR	Bromley	Brighton	BN
BS	Bristol	Bristol	BS
BT	Belfast	Bromley	BR
CA	Carlisle	Cambridge	CB
CB	Cambridge	Canterbury	CT
CF	Cardiff	Cardiff	CF
CH	Chester	Carlisle	CA
CM	Chelmsford	Chelmsford	CM
CO	Colchester	Chester	CH
CR	Croydon	Colchester	CO
CT	Canterbury	Coventry	CV
CV	Coventry	Crewe	CW
CW	Crewe	Croydon	CR
DA	Dartford	Darlington	DL
DD	Dundee	Dartford	DA
DE	Derby	Derby	DE
DG	Dumfries	Doncaster	DN
DH	Durham	Dorchester	DT
DL	Darlington	Dudley	DY
DN	Doncaster	Dumfries	DG
DT	Dorchester	Dundee	DD
DY	Dudley	Durham	DH
E	London E	Edinburgh	EH
EC	London EC	Enfield	EN
EH	Edinburgh	Exeter	EX
EN	Enfield	Falkirk	FK
EX	Exeter	Galashiels	TD
FK	Falkirk	Glasgow	G
FY	Blackpool	Gloucester	GL
G	Glasgow	Guildford	GU
GL	Gloucester	Halifax	HX
GU	Guildford	Harrogate	HG

Tony's Guide

to the courier industry

HA	Harrow	Harrow	HA
HD	Huddersfield	Hebrides	HS
HG	Harrogate	Hemel Hempstead	HP
HP	Hemel Hempstead	Hereford	HR
HR	Hereford	Huddersfield	HD
HS	Hebrides	Ilford	IG
HU	Kingston upon Hull	Inverness	IV
HX	Halifax	Ipswich	IP
IG	Ilford	Isle of Man	IM
IM	Isle of Man	Kilmarnock	KA
IP	Ipswich	Kingston upon Hull	HU
		Kingston-upon-	
IV	Inverness	Thames	KT
KA	Kilmarnock	Kirkcaldy	KY
	Kingston-upon-		
KT	Thames	Kirkwall	KW
KW	Kirkwall	Lancaster	LA
KY	Kirkcaldy	Leeds	LS
L	Liverpool	Leicester	LE
LA	Lancaster	Lerwick	ZE
LD	Llandrindod Wells	Lincoln	LN
LE	Leicester	Liverpool	L
LL	Llandudno	Llandrindod Wells	LD
LN	Lincoln	Llandudno	LL
LS	Leeds	London E	E
LU	Luton	London EC	EC
M	Manchester	London N	N
ME	Medway	London NW	NW
MK	Milton Keynes	London SE	SE
ML	Motherwell	London SW	SW
N	London N	London W	W

Tony's Guide

NE	Newcastle upon Tyne	London WC	WC
NG	Nottingham	Luton	LU
NN	Northampton	Manchester	M
NP	Newport	Medway	ME
NR	Norwich	Milton Keynes	MK
NW	London NW	Motherwell	ML
OL	Oldham	Newcastle upon Tyne	NE
OX	Oxford	Newport	NP
PO	Portsmouth	Northampton	NN
PA	Paisley	Norwich	NR
PE	Peterborough	Nottingham	NG
PH	Perth	Oldham	OL
PL	Plymouth	Oxford	OX
PR	Preston	Paisley	PA
RG	Reading	Perth	PH
RH	Redhill	Peterborough	PE
RM	Romford	Plymouth	PL
S	Sheffield	Portsmouth	PO
SA	Swansea	Preston	PR
SE	London SE	Reading	RG
SG	Stevenage	Redhill	RH
SK	Stockport	Romford	RM
SL	Slough	Royal Tunbridge Wells	TN
SM	Sutton	Salisbury	SP
SN	Swindon	Sheffield	S
SO	Southampton	Shrewsbury	SY
SP	Salisbury	Slough	SL
SR	Sunderland	Southall	UB
SS	Southend-on-Sea	Southampton	SO
ST	Stoke-on-Trent	Southend-on-Sea	SS
SW	London SW	St Albans	AL
SY	Shrewsbury	Stevenage	SG
TA	Taunton	Stockport	SK

Tony's Guide

TD	Galashiels	Stoke-on-Trent	ST
TF	Telford	Sunderland	SR
TN	Royal Tunbridge Wells	Sutton	SM
TQ	Torquay	Swansea	SA
TR	Truro	Swindon	SN
TS	Teesside	Taunton	TA
TW	Twickenham	Teesside	TS
UB	Southall	Telford	TF
W	London W	Torquay	TQ
WA	Warrington	Truro	TR
WC	London WC	Twickenham	TW
WD	Watford	Wakefield	WF
WF	Wakefield	Walsall	WS
WN	Wigan	Warrington	WA
WR	Worcester	Watford	WD
WS	Walsall	Wigan	WN
WV	Wolverhampton	Wolverhampton	WV
YO	York	Worcester	WR
ZE	Lerwick	York	YO

Tony's Guide

Tony's Guide
to the courier industry

Here are some suggestions:

The XDAII from O2 has a camera, and fast access to the internet.

The Sony P910 is available from Orange.

You can install satnav on both of these.

We recommend that you look carefully at the SatNav system available from **www.Wayfinder.com**. It runs only on mobiles with a "Symbian" operating system (eg Nokia and Sony handsets), and is very good value.

In our opinion, every courier should have some kind of internet access in the van, as a basic tool of the trade.

You can tell MTvan.com where and when you will be empty, so MTvan.com can send you text messages about nearby work during the day.

It also helps to team up with other Members to keep an eye on MTvan.com for each other.

© Tim Gilbert 2005

Tony's Guide

to the courier industry

You might be able to use some of this Mission Statement in your courier business.

Who we are

<Name> Couriers, established in <year>, is a privately owned company specialising in same day express courier despatch by bicycle, motorbike and van. We have couriers operating throughout the UK. We have an established reputation for quality among a broad customer base.

How we want the world to see us

We aim to be recognised as:

The courier company whom all potential customers and particularly Plc's can trust to handle their courier contracts.
The principal courier service to the <chosen sector> industry in the UK.
The courier company with far and away the most efficient accounts department in the industry.
The company the best couriers will queue to work for.
The company to approach if you want to sell your courier business.

Our everyday activities

In our everyday activities, we aim always to remember the basics:

To answer the phone quickly and with our first name.

To collect the goods quickly
To deliver quickly and to obtain a clear signature.
To pay our couriers a viable rate accurately, promptly and informatively.
To invoice our customers accurately and informatively and for a fair price.
To resolve queries quickly and cheerfully.
To collect the money politely and firmly.

Our expansion plans

We believe that by sticking to the basics on an everyday level, we will always have the strong foundations on which to expand. We aim to grow both by reputation and sheer hard work into all available profitable markets.

Our Training policy

We believe that training our staff improves both customer service and job satisfaction. We train our people in accordance with our Training Schedule.

The way we use money

Financially we aim:

To keep borrowings to a minimum and short term.
To remain within a declared range of current ratio on a strong balance sheet.
To grow within our own means.
To reward effort, talent and success in our staff with fair and reliable pay and an exciting and secure future in a profitable and expanding company.

To pay our creditors within 30 days of the end of the month of receipt, and thereby to obtain both the best price and the best service from our suppliers.

Our environmental policy

We aim to be profitable at least cost to the environment. We have a written environment policy.

Where we are going

We aim to remain a strong and well-managed company, which is best placed to profit from our core same-day express courier activities for as long as this remains a worthwhile market.
We are also committed to finding new and equally dynamic core activities for the 21st century.

© Tim Gilbert 2005

Tony's Guide

to the courier industry

Tony's Guide

to the courier industry

[You should consult your lawyer to ensure that they are suitable for your needs, before using them in your business].

These are sample terms and conditions of carriage. You should check with your solicitor and other professional advisors before relying on them.

It is important that your customer are fully aware of them before you do any work for them.

They should appear on the back of a hard copy account application form. If you wish to start up an account immediately, your terms may not be binding the customer has seen them first.

1   Definitions

"We,Us,Our" shall refer to [your business name]

"You,Your,Yours" shall refer to the customer with whom We contract with for the carriage of Goods;

"Goods" shall be the Goods which are the subject of the contract for carriage;

"Conditions" means terms and conditions of carriage.

2   Our Obligations

© Tim Gilbert 2005

2.1   We shall carry, store and transport the Goods from the collection address specified by You at the time of booking by such routes, means or procedures as We in Our absolute discretion consider appropriate.

2.2   We may employ, instruct or entrust the performance of all or part of the contract to others.

3   Your Obligations

3.1   You expressly warrant that the Goods are Yours or that You are the owner or the owner's authorised agent and that You are authorised to accept and do accept the Conditions for yourselves but also as agents for and on behalf of any other person who may have rights in the Goods.

3.2   You warrant that all Goods entrusted to Us for carriage have been properly and sufficiently packed, labelled and/or prepared and that the Goods are suitable for carriage in the vehicle provided by Us.

3.3   All accounts will be rendered by Us at least monthly and You will settle Your account in full within 30 days of the date of the invoice and You will not make any deductions or withhold any payments on account of any claim, counterclaim or setoff.

4   Risk

4.1   Subject to the provisions of these Conditions the Goods will be at Our risk the time they are delivered to Us or collected by Us until the Goods have been delivered or tendered for delivery at the delivery address or, where We are to hold the Goods for collection or further instructions, until one working day has elapsed since We have notified You or the designated consignee of the availability of the Goods.

5   <u>Our Liability</u>

5.1   We shall be liable for:

(a)   loss of or damage to the Goods;
(b)   delay or error in delivery of the Goods;
(c)   failure to follow any reasonable instructions which we have agreed with.

Providing that it is reasonably proved that the loss, damage, non-delivery or mis-delivery was due to Our negligence or default (or that of our employees).

5.2   Apart from as stated above and liability for death or personal injury arising from Our negligence (or that of our employees or agents) We shall be under no liability whatsoever in connection with the Goods or any instructions, advice, information or otherwise.
5.3   No expressions of acceptance of any responsibility made by any of Our employees or agents shall be in fact admissions unless confirmed by Our managing director.

5.4   We shall not, under any circumstances, be liable for any detention or delay of the Goods or any consequential loss, damage or deterioration arising from it except where:

(a)   You have specified the nature of the Goods and the purposes for which they are required and We have agreed in writing a time schedule specification for those Goods; and
(b)   it is proved that the potential loss, delay, damage or deterioration was due to Our negligence.

6   <u>Limitations</u>

© Tim Gilbert 2005

6.1   For carriage within Great Britain (excluding Northern Ireland and any off shore islands) by a bicycle, motorcycle, or van ordered by You and provided by Us, Our liability shall not exceed the value of the relevant Goods or the sum of [£5,000] per Consignment whichever is the lesser in accordance with Our Goods in Transit insurance policy.

6.2   For an international delivery ordered by You and provided by Us Our liability shall not exceed:

(a)   the value of the relevant Goods; or
(b)   a sum at the rate of [£800] per tonne or 1,000 kilos on the gross weight of the Goods;
whichever is the lesser provided that Our minimum liability will be [£50] in respect of any Consignment.

6.3   For an international delivery ordered by you and provided by an agent or subcontractor of Ours, Our liability shall be limited to the amount that We are able to claim for such agent or sub-contractor for any loss or damage.

6.4   We shall not accept any claims for loss or damage relating to Goods or non-delivery or mis-delivery unless We are advised of a claim in writing within 7 working days of the date of the Consignment and the claim is quantified within 28 days from the date of the Consignment.

7   Exclusions from carriage

7.1   We will not accept or deal with any noxious, dangerous, hazardous or inflammable or explosive Goods or any Goods likely to cause such damage or any valuable or fragile goods (and by way of illustration only the Goods listed in Schedule A below) without special arrangement in writing With Us. Should You nevertheless, deliver any such Goods to Us or cause Us to handle or deal with any such

Goods You will be liable for <u>all</u> loss or damage whatsoever caused by or to or in connection with those Goods and shall indemnify Us against all penalties, claims, damages, costs and expenses arising in connection with the Goods. We shall be under no liability whatsoever in connection with such Goods. We may destroy such Goods or otherwise dispose of them at Our sole discretion and at Your cost.

8   General

8.1   If any legislation is compulsorily applicable to any contract undertaken these Conditions shall be read in such context as subject to the legislation provided that nothing shall be taken as a surrender by Us of any of Our rights or immunities or as an increase of Our responsibilities or liabilities under any relevant legislation.

8.2   If any part of these conditions be void or unlawful under any relevant law or legislation the relevant clause or portion or the clause shall disregard it without effect to any other clause or part of the conditions.

8.3   We are not a common carrier and We only transact business on these terms. No terms or conditions proposed by or referred to You in writing or otherwise shall form part of this contract unless agreed to in writing signed by one of Our directors.

8.4   All agreements made between Us and You shall be governed by English law and shall be subject to the non-exclusive jurisdiction of the English courts.

Schedule 1

Excluded Goods

Tony's Guide
to the courier industry

Bullion, coins, precious stones, jewellery, valuables, antiques, pictures, furniture, securities, deeds, bills of exchange, promissory notes, documents of title to property, stamps, photographs, cassettes, videos, spirits, tobacco and cigarettes, brittle, fragile or breakable articles, non-ferrous metals other than in component form, human or animal remains, food stuffs, drugs, furs, nuclear fuel or nuclear waste.

Tony's Guide

This section describes the different roles of people in a small to medium sized courier business, and makes suggestions as to what you should expect from anyone who takes on any of these roles.

You may find these useful when employing people to fill these roles. Employing people can be a risky business, so you should take professional advice before applying anything you read here to your business.

Business Owner - Principal Responsibilities

To maintain high standards of service throughout the day to day operations of their office by implementing and maintaining company policy. To maintain the discipline, loyalty and morale of staff. To ensure a high standard of customer care. To maintain profit margins. To train ad sustain adequate levels of high quality freelance couriers. To maintain charge rates at their optimum regional level. Keeping bad debts to a minimum through constant vigilance. To maintain a clean and professional, uncluttered working environment.

Tony's Guide

Principal Daily Elements:

- ❑ opening up office in the morning

- ❑ call-taking and booking jobs

- ❑ controlling jobs and couriers

- ❑ dealing with customer enquiries or complaints

- ❑ POD entry

- ❑ phoning customers with POD's and other information

- ❑ checking previous days data

- ❑ managing office staff and couriers

- ❑ closing down operation in evening

Summary

The role is to run the office such that each job from booking to completed delivery is completed with a maximum of speed and efficiency - thus guaranteeing the loyalty and future business of each customer.

Role of Office Manager

Accountable to:
The Business Owner

Tony's Guide
to the courier industry

Accountable For:

- ❏ Achieving your performance targets in respect of sales and profits.
- ❏ Ensuring the provision of an efficient courier service to the standard specified in the Operating Manual.
- ❏ Ensuring that all property and equipment owned by your business is maintained in first class condition and operating at optimum efficiency.
- ❏ Ensuring that all branch employees and couriers are aware of their responsibilities and the contribution required of them by your business, and are competent and motivated to do what your business requires them to do.
- ❏ Providing accurate and comprehensive management information to the Business Owner services as and when required.
- ❏ Ensuring the branch and all its staff project a favourable and appropriate company image at all times.
- ❏ Ensuring that there are sufficient trained couriers of the right calibre to service the anticipated needs of the branch.
- ❏ Ensuring the branch and its staff, including the couriers, operate strictly in accordance with company policy, instructions and guidelines at all times.

Contribution

- ❏ To generate income by achieving profitable sales in line with specified goals and targets through the use of sound management practices.
- ❏ To enhance profitability by ensuring the efficient use of time, material and manpower resources.
- ❏ To increase profitability by creating a favourable image of the business and encouraging repeat business and referrals.
- ❏ To add value by improving the skills, competencies and attitudes of employees, including couriers.

Outputs

- ❏ Profitable Sales in line with specified targets.
- ❏ Efficient courier services for customers.
- ❏ Management information, data and market intelligence.
- ❏ Support, direction, co-ordination, and motivation of all personnel, including couriers.

Inputs

- ❑ Company Policy, corporate and marketing strategy.
- ❑ Performance targets and directions issued by the Business Owner
- ❑ Necessary physical, financial and other resources.
- ❑ Internal & external advice, support and training.
- ❑ Market intelligence, data and information.
- ❑ Administrative support.
- ❑ The personal skills and attributes identified by your business on recruitment and enhanced by a programme of continuous personal development.
- ❑ Adequate time and freedom from distractions. This may necessitate the purchase of additional time; i.e. additional manpower resources.

Role of the Salesman

Accountable to
Branch Manager, National Sales Manager

Accountable For

- ❑ Achieving sales targets by generating new business and maintaining existing business.
- ❑ Implementing your business's marketing and selling strategy in your catchment area.
- ❑ Devising and implementing a Sales Plan that will achieve your targets
- ❑ Providing accurate management information
- ❑ Ensuring the definitive company story is delivered to and received by every qualified business in the area in the form specified by you.
- ❑ Ensuring that selling skills within the branch are of a highly professional standard and constantly updated.
- ❑ Creating and maintaining a strong and favourable company image throughout the area at all times.

Contribution

- ❑ To generate income by achieving profitable sales in line with specified goals and targets.
- ❑ To enhance profitability by the efficient use of time, skill and other available resources.
- ❑ To increase profitability by creating a favourable image of the business and encouraging repeat business and referrals.

Tony's Guide

Outputs

- ❑ Profitable sales in line with specified targets.
- ❑ Management information, data and market intelligence.
- ❑ Enquiries and other selling opportunities.

Inputs

- ❑ Company Policy, corporate and marketing strategy.
- ❑ Management information and directions specified by the branch manager, and the Business Owner
- ❑ Necessary physical, financial and other resources.
- ❑ Internal and external advice, support and training.
- ❑ Market intelligence, data and information.
- ❑ Administrative support.
- ❑ The personal skills and attributes identified by your business on recruitment and enhanced by a programme of continuous personal development.
- ❑ Adequate time and freedom from distractions. This may necessitate the purchase of additional time; i.e. additional manpower resources.

Role of Call Taker:

Accountable to
Office Manager

Accountable For

- ❏ Ensuring total customer satisfaction by providing and efficient and reliable courier service that meets or exceeds their expectations.
- ❏ Implementing and enforcing your business's operating system and standards.
- ❏ Ensuring consistently high standards of appearance and performance from couriers and vehicles.
- ❏ Providing accurate information as, when and in the form required by the business owner.
- ❏ Maintaining effective communications and records.
- ❏ Ensuring a strong and favourable company image is constantly sustained and projected by branch operations and all couriers.

Contribution

- ❏ To generate income by ensuring that all packages are collected and delivered exactly in accordance with customer requirements.
- ❏ To enhance profitability by the efficient use of time, skill and other available resources.
- ❏ To increase profitability by creating a favourable image of the business and encouraging repeat business and referrals.

Tony's Guide

Outputs

- Movement of packages from source to destination.
- Instructions to couriers.
- Organisation and training of couriers.
- Communications with customers and other branches.
- Management information, data and market intelligence.

Inputs

- Enquiries and instructions from customers
- Reports and calls from couriers.
- Company policy, corporate and marketing strategy.
- Performance targets and directions specified by the branch manager and head office.
- Necessary physical, financial and other resources.
- Internal and external advice, support and training.
- Administrative support.
- The personal skills and attributes identified by your business on recruitment and enhanced by a programme of continuous personal development.
- Adequate time and freedom from distractions. This may necessitate the purchase of additional time; i.e. additional manpower resources.

© Tim Gilbert 2005

Tony's Guide

to the courier industry

MTvan.com offers business training covering the following aspects of running a courier company, at our HQ in St Ives Cambridgeshire.

❑ **Courier Management**

This seminar is given by a member of MTvan.com, who has first hand experience of running a Courier Office. The seminar lasts ½ day and will cover:

❑ Recruiting and Managing staff and couriers

❑ How to prepare adverts to get staff and couriers

❑ Interviewing couriers and how to handle couriers

❑ Using MTvan.com to find extra couriers

❑ Using MTvan.com to get PODs from your couriers

❑ Customer Care

❑ Sales and Marketing

This seminar is given by a member of MTvan.com's staff experienced as a courier sales person. It lasts one day. The purpose of this seminar is to go through the basics of Sales and Marketing, Customer Care, and Telephone Technique. Some time spent is also on managing sales people, including how to recruit the people necessary to take the business to where you want it to go.

❑ Finance and Administration

This section of the training lasts ½ day and is co-ordinated by the financial controller of MTvan.com.

Call (without obligation) for prices on 01480 309347.

Tony's Guide

to the courier industry

Tony's Guide

to the courier industry

The author of this manual is available to solve problems you may have in your courier business, on a consultancy basis. Call (without obligation) Tim Gilbert on 01480 309347.

© Tim Gilbert 2005

Tony's Guide

"Neither a wise man nor a brave man lies down on the tracks of history to wait for the train of the future to run over him"
-    DWIGHT D. EISENHOWER.

Tony's Guide
to the courier industry

Tony's Guide
to the courier industry

"A pessimist sees the difficulty in every opportunity; an optimist sees the opportunity in every difficulty".
- SIR WINSTON CHURCHILL

ISBN 141202400-5